This book is dedicated to parents and educators around the world who encourage meaningful communication – and to the children who will one day use that communication to make a more peaceful, loving world.

baby signers

If you'd like to learn more about joining a class or becoming a
Babysigners teacher, visit **www.babysigners.co.uk**.

Babysigners is a UK-based teaching network that runs baby-signing classes
founded upon the principles laid down by Dr Joseph Garcia.

A Babysigners Publication from Match Media Publishing Limited,
77 Walton Street, London SW3 2HT, United Kingdom

First printing 2005

ISBN: 1-904840-00-0

Editor: Julie Postance
UK baby-signing consultant: Emma Finlay-Smith
British Sign Language (BSL) consultant: Erika James
Design: Mears Ash
Illustration: Richard, Christine and James Deverell
DVD design: Four Corners Media
Publishing consultants: Simon Dwyer, Alex Slater

Contents

About the author

Dr Joseph Garcia is one of the world's foremost experts on communicating with infants. In his highly acclaimed books Toddler Talk (1994) and SIGN with your BABY (1999), Dr Garcia explores the miracle of how babies as young as seven months are able to communicate with their parents using signing. This, Garcia's latest book, is the culmination of his research and experience as a teacher and of his extensive work with more than 5,000 babies and their families since 1986. His exciting new approach will help parents and caregivers find it easy to learn and use more signs than they thought possible – while having a lot of fun.

Editorial note by the author

A baby is either a boy or a girl. That means that technically a baby ought to be described as 'him or her', 'he or she', 'himself or herself' – which can be highly intrusive in sentences that include a number of such references. Accordingly, I have followed the customary practice of referring to either 'him' or 'her', but not both, and consistently one or the other per chapter.

Part I

Discovering the joys of baby signing

What is baby signing?

Welcome

Congratulations on taking this, your first important step towards opening up a whole new world of communication with your baby. For those of us who have already discovered it, communicating with our babies before they can speak is one of the most life-changing experiences we could ever have. Seeing your baby signing for the first time is every bit as enthralling as hearing her articulate her first words or watching her take her first steps.

Your baby's first two years of life are a multitude of marvels, mysteries and magic moments. Most of what she experiences is fresh and unfamiliar: she explores every face, object, and feeling with an innate inquisitiveness. To remain a passive observer of this thrilling new world is simply not enough for her. Your baby is a highly social creature, for whom transference of thought is a normal and essential part of life. She is born with a natural desire to communicate, and she makes the most of whatever means she has in an effort to share her thoughts and feelings with you through facial expressions, body language and vocal sounds. However, her understanding of the world around her and her desire to express her understanding far exceed her capabilities to communicate at this early age.

All parents know the frustration that results when their babies cry for something and when intuition and guesswork fail to resolve the issue. The anxiety we as caregivers experience when we cannot figure out our children's needs can be heartrending. This situation continues until our children can learn to articulate and use the words they need to express themselves. The point at which babies can use their voices to tell you what is on their little minds can range anywhere between 12 months and two years. And the number of words children gain command over varies dramatically from a few simple words to many. There is also the issue of clarity and enunciation as their little voices learn to make the sounds correctly.

Imagine how you would feel if your baby could explain that she was hungry, needed her nappy changed or wanted her favourite teddy bear. What if there was a method that could offer her a way to communicate well before she could utter her first word? What if this method could enable her to indicate exactly what she wanted or needed, prevent frustration, reduce tantrums and remove much of the misery resulting from miscommunication or non-communication? What if there was a method that would offer you a whole new insight into the way she actually perceives the world?

There is a method that does all that.

It is called baby signing. It can reduce frustration, tantrums and misery, and – best of all – it can help you gain insight into your baby's world long before speech begins.

So what is baby signing?

Often, when the term 'baby signing' is mentioned to parents, they associate it with children who are hearing-impaired. But baby signing is for all parents and caregivers, and it is for all babies, both with and without hearing difficulties. It is simply an effective and loving way to communicate with your baby before she can talk.

Baby signs are simple gestures that you add to your normal speech when you are talking to your baby. Gestures that allow her to communicate before she has mastered the complexity of spoken language. From the age of about seven months – long before her speech has developed – the muscles in her hands are sufficiently formed to enable her to make gestures. When she 'waves goodbye' or shrugs her shoulders, she is demonstrating her ability to do this. Baby signing is just a natural extension of what she already finds very easy to do.

Baby signing's greatest benefit is that it allows your child to express herself clearly. Introducing just a few simple signs into your baby's life allows her painlessly and effortlessly to enlighten you of her wants and needs. The signs remove the distress and the need to cry in order to get what she wants. And most importantly, when this tool is at your fingertips you will enjoy many unforgettable conversations you would have missed had you waited until she was able to talk.

Baby signing bridging the communication gap – Joseph and daughter Alaina sign 'telephone'

You do not have to learn the whole language to gain this wonderful advantage. Just a few signs will permit the two of you to engage in 'conversation' together. There is no need to teach her the signs – just demonstrate them to her (add them to your speech) as you go about your daily routine. She will observe them and eventually, through daily exposure, begin to mimic what she sees. When she understands that the signs mean something specific, she will begin to use these signs in order to get what she desires. With time and use, simple signs will be added together until she is creating sentences. During her first two years she will be able to build up a large vocabulary of signs that far surpass the number of words she could ever articulate to be understood at that age.

All this activity will assist your baby in organising her thoughts into language. Later, as her vocal ability develops, she will begin to use the words she heard with each sign and transfer her signing language skills to her new and developing speech. That is why you say the word simultaneously with the sign – so that your baby can connect the word with the sign and the concept behind each sign/word.

Where does it come from?

For many years scientists, doctors, researchers and educators have studied sign language as a means to assist communication in children with hearing or speech impairments and other special needs, such as Down's syndrome and autism. However, the idea of using signing with hearing babies to enhance communication has been largely neglected until relatively recently.

My fascination with sign language began as a child at school when I observed hearing-impaired children and hearing children of deaf parents using signs to communicate. One interesting mystery that stuck with me was that the children who were raised in a signing family seemed to have competent, if not advanced, language skills – despite being raised in a strict signing environment.

Later in life, I began to work as a sign language interpreter and instructor. As a hearing person, my language skills and close association with deaf friends allowed me to learn about the limitless beauty of their language and the art and depth of their culture. I saw something among the Deaf community that helped me solve the mystery from my childhood. I saw that hearing (as well as deaf) babies raised in a signing environment were able to clearly communicate through signs much earlier than the average child without exposure to signs. I also noticed that the hearing children who signed had better vocabularies and used words more effectively than non-signing children at similar ages.

This second glimpse at signs being used in the first stages of language acquisition caused me to ponder over the value that signs might have in invoking the concept and use of language in very young children. In 1987 I began studying child development and language acquisition at Alaska Pacific University. For my thesis I chose to research the use of American Sign Language (ASL) with hearing babies of hearing parents. Although a great deal of research had been conducted in the area of using sign language with deaf children, I struggled to find any studies that referred to using sign language with hearing babies. There was a small amount of research on hearing children of deaf parents, but the focus was pretty much always on speech acquisition by deaf or hard-of-hearing children. Indeed, back then, the idea of improving language in hearing babies through signs was almost inconceivable, much less popular. I was in new territory.

I conducted a research study involving 17 infants and their parents. My study revealed that when these babies were regularly exposed to signs from seven months of age, they were able to communicate with signs as early as the eighth month.

At the same time that I was researching, Dr Linda Acredolo and Dr Susan Goodwyn of the University of California were also examining the use of gestural communication between hearing parents and babies. Their findings prompted them to launch an ongoing research programme that has since lasted 20 years and generated a wealth of published research, much of it funded by the US National Institute of Health. In contrast, my emphasis was on understanding the delivery process which would maximise the potential that signs could provide in pre-speech communication.

Despite conducting our research at the same time, we remained unaware of each other's work. At any rate, the purposes of our two research projects were very different. Whereas Acredolo and Goodwyn were trying to demonstrate that babies could sign, and that signing wouldn't harm them, I was developing an effective teaching method to facilitate what I knew from years of firsthand experience – that signing with babies was enormously beneficial as a method of communication, and that when approached correctly, this method could be a valuable asset during the elementary stages of language acquisition. The issues I faced were to convince hearing people that signs were indeed valuable, and to create a readily usable system for an already overwhelmed parent that was easy and that worked.

After graduation, I began developing such a system of sign language for parents and their pre-speech babies, and in 1994 I published my first book on the subject entitled *Toddler Talk*. In 1996 the Acredolo and Goodwyn team published their book, *Baby Signs*, which advocated the use of invented signs rather than standardised signs.

When I commenced my doctoral studies in adult learning and education, I improved and enlarged my programme, which is now known as *SIGN with your BABY*. Following its 1999 publication, it became the world's leading baby-signing programme and has been used to enhance communication between parents and their babies in hundreds of thousands of families.

Introducing my latest programme

Since then, I've been deeply involved in communication research and expanding caregiver knowledge of baby signing. My personal focus remains on creating the most effective and practical signing methods for parents and babies. The fundamentals of my original methods still apply because they apply to all language acquisition. However, my studies, observations and firsthand experiences over the past fifteen years have provided me with a wealth of additional insights that inspired me to write this book.

I call this book *The Complete Guide to Baby Signing* because it not only reveals the theory behind baby signing but it also clearly demonstrates how to incorporate the signs into your everyday activities. It is grounded on what I term the 'topic-learning' method that assists you in using a relatively large number of signs based on daily routines. My programme can teach you – in a fun and stress-free way – how to learn a small or a large number of signs with your baby. Investing a great deal of time is not necessary – just a few signs can make a world of difference. Your child will then be able to discover and use these signs through consistent daily exposure. Having already tried and tested these methods with thousands of families, I have been able to produce results which show that parents and their children are now learning and using more signs than ever before.

This book is written specifically for British parents and is based on British Sign Language, although, in some instances I have modified several of the signs with advanced movements to make them easier for your baby to produce.

How to use this book

For you to obtain an overall understanding and appreciation of what is involved in baby signing, I recommend that you read the book in its entirety. However, if you want to get straight into learning how to sign, please do feel free to move straight to the Golden rules in Chapter 5. The book is divided into four Parts. Part I provides background information on what baby signing actually is, why it works, and its origins and benefits. It also features the seven major benefits of baby signing and an introduction to get you started. Part II provides useful signs, grouped according to your daily routines, and a wealth of games, books and rhymes. Part III covers every other question you have ever wanted an answer to about baby signing, as well as solutions to any of the issues you may encounter on your way. Part IV contains an A to Z of 172 signs. There is also an Invented signs page at the back on which to record your own personal signs and their origins.

You will notice that I refer to your baby as 'he' or as 'she' in alternating chapters: this is just a convention writers use to give the sexes equal attention.

The greatest gift

Learning anything new as an adult takes a certain degree of courage, and I applaud you for stepping out of your comfort zone to learn more about this fascinating subject. Before you embark on this adventure, let me remind you that baby signing will require from you a degree of patience. Baby signing does not happen overnight – your baby's first signs will take time to appear but when they do, the payoffs will far surpass your expectations and lead you to the same sense of exhilaration reported to me by the thousands of families who have gone before you.

The many years I have worked in the field of infant communication have strengthened my conviction that there is no greater gift you can bestow on your child than the ability to communicate. I wish you well on your baby-signing journey and trust that you and your baby have tremendous fun together as you help bring out the best in her.

"Do you want something to eat?" Joseph asks his daughter Alaina

MY BABY-SIGNING BOOK

My name is _____

I was born on _____

Insert a photo of your baby signing here

My first sign was _____

I made it on _____

My most memorable signing moment was

_____

_____

_____

_____

How baby signing can dramatically improve your life and your baby's

What is at the heart of this baby-signing revolution? Why would you use signs with your baby? During my many years of researching and teaching baby signing, I have received countless reports from overjoyed parents and other caregivers on the positive effects of signing. My own experiences with my children also helped me to understand the incredible benefit that signing offers young babies. Each story I hear, although unique, reinforces the fact that there are a multitude of reasons for introducing signing into your life – reasons that have immense implications for a more harmonious life with your child.

True Story

When my daughter Lauren was just seven months old, she learned how to ask for more milk. Before long, she could tell us that she wanted a nap, that her tummy was sore or that her nappy needed changing. Signing has been a godsend. Chris and I were so used to running through the nappy, dummy, milk checklist until she'd stopped crying. It's certainly changed our relationship with her and made parenting a lot more fun. It's made a massive difference with the carers at her nursery – they don't have to endure the tears and guessing games with Lauren that they are used to from the other toddlers. For me, the greatest joy is knowing what's going on inside her head and being able to give her exactly what she wants.

Baby-signing mum Phillipa, Gloucestershire

Expert opinion

Perhaps the largest study to date has been conducted by Californian psychologists Dr Linda Acredolo and Dr Susan Goodwyn, and funded by the National Institute for Child Health and Human Development in the USA. Commencing in July 2000, it observed 140 families over two years, during which time the differences were noted between babies who had been taught sign language and those who had not.

At the end of two years, the study showed that the children who used signs not only talked at an earlier age but also comprehended more of what was communicated to them and had broader vocabularies than their non-signing peers. Their developmental play was more advanced and they demonstrated a greater desire to read books. Parents of the signers reported increased communication between them and their children, less frustration, fewer tantrums and an improved relationship between themselves and their babies.

The seven main benefits of baby signing

Similar tendencies have been reported among children who sign. The most obvious benefits are that it:

1 provides your baby with the ability to communicate his wants, needs and observations before he can talk

2 reduces your and your baby's frustration and reduces the number and duration of tantrums

3 offers you a whole new insight into your baby's world

4 strengthens the bond between you and your baby

5 increases your baby's confidence

6 accelerates your baby's language development so that when speech begins, the content is more sophisticated

7 fuels intellectual development.

Let's examine these seven benefits one at a time.

Benefit 1:

Baby signing enhances communication

Your baby understands language long before he can talk. At around seven to ten months old he is beginning to recognise what is going on around him and is eager to communicate with you. In the absence of an effective way to express himself, his only form of communication is babbling, smiling, whining or crying.

Using sign language, your baby no longer has to ride the rollercoaster of life with no control over his environment. With sign literally at his fingertips, he can bridge the gap between spoken language and comprehension. He acquires the ability to communicate clearly and accurately what he desires, and can be understood by you and by others. He attains the power to initiate real conversations and convey his delights and qualms, without the tears.

True Story

With the help of signing, my daughter Isabelle would let me know her needs – for instance, if she was tired and wanted to go to bed or needed help. Once when she was 13 months old, she uncharacteristically awoke me in the middle of the night, wailing. When I went into her bedroom, she signed HOT and then MEDICINE. Sure enough, her temperature was very high. After I gave her some medicine, she lay down happily and went back to sleep. How wonderful it was that she could tell me what she needed long before she could talk! She's now just two years old and talks all the time – much more so than her two-year-old friends.

Baby-signing mum Gemma, Putney

Benefit 2:

Baby signing reduces frustration and reduces the number and duration of tantrums

Frustration usually arises as a result of unfulfilled expectations. No matter how good a parent you are, you will never anticipate your baby's every wish because his desire to communicate is so often thwarted by your inability to understand him. The first two years of his life can be intensely exasperating, and a little later in life 'the terrible twos' are partly a result of his frustration. Much of this frustration comes from restricted communication and from being misunderstood.

However, frustration levels drop dramatically when he learns how to sign. With a means to express himself, he is able to convey his needs swiftly and calmly and with a minimum of fuss.

True Story

During the school holidays my 18-month-old Kieran really loves having the chance to play with his older brother and sister in the garden. Early one morning I was just about to send him out to play with them when he became distressed. I asked him if he wanted to go out to play and he shook his head, making the sign for SLEEP. Had he not been able to sign, I would never have known that he was tired and would have sent him outside. Instead, I put him to bed and he slept for two hours. It's been wonderful not having to guess what Kieran wants – we all know how frustrating that can be.

Baby-signing mum Tracy, Reading

Nothing sets children off quicker than a parent's saying 'no' to something they want without offering them a reason, explanation or possible alternative. Baby signing assists parents in providing an alternative to the word 'no'. If my children wanted a biscuit before dinner, I would say/sign, 'When you have FINISHED EATING.' If they wanted to watch a movie before bathtime, I would say/sign, 'Yes, you can watch the movie when you have FINISHED having a BATH.' Each time their request was acknowledged, but it was clear that they had to do something first in order to have their request fulfilled. I found, with time, that there were fewer tantrums and confrontations.

Parents and caregivers can often eliminate frustration and the resulting crying fits with simple communication. I appreciate that intuitive parents are often able to read their baby's cries without resorting to signals. Yet baby signing moves beyond just suppressing crying towards more accurately establishing what a baby needs. Signs minimise the guesswork and so, in turn, free up time for more positive interactions with the child. There is something wonderful about witnessing a signing family communicating together in a warm, easy and natural way.

It is not only immediate family members who get the benefit of reduced frustration levels. British Sign Language is becoming more and more a standard part of pre-school curricula because it minimises stress for children and for professional caregivers who must respond to the needs of several children at a time.

Nursery staff have reported lower noise intensities when infants use signing rather than resorting to deafening screams or crying. They also say that signing significantly reduces incidences of negative behaviour such as lying on the floor, hitting and biting. Through signs infants learn concepts like being GENTLE and SHARING at an early age, and therefore begin to understand kindness and cooperation.

Expert Opinion

Dr Kimberly Whaley started a longitudinal study in November 1999 to research the use of ASL signs with pre-verbal babies in a pre-school environment. After her pilot study – conducted at Ohio State's A. Sophie Rogers Infant Toddler Laboratory School – she noted:

'It is so much easier for our teachers to work with 12-month-olds who can sign that they want their bottle rather than just cry and have us try to figure out what they want. This is a great way for infants to express their needs before they can verbalise them.'

Benefit 3:

Baby signing provides a whole new insight into your baby's world

How unfortunate it is that some people limit their engagement with children because young babies do not have much to offer by way of conversation. This misconception is not the babies' fault. Just because babies cannot talk does not mean that they do not have a great deal to talk about. Your baby's first two years are a wonderful, miraculous adventure. It is a time when he discovers a whole new world of exciting people, things and places and is eager to share his new knowledge with you.

With baby signing he can tell you what he sees, thinks and feels, and what holds his interest. He can tell you that he is afraid of something or that he wants you to do something he likes again and again. It allows you a unique insight into his mind and his personality. It reveals some of the mysteries of babyhood.

With baby signing he can point out to you, with fascination and excitement, the world that you often take for granted – the kind old lady in the shop, the kite high in the sky and the spider hanging from a thread in the garden. It will enable you to see the world with new eyes and offer you a new or revived appreciation for life in general.

True Story

Signing with Ethan has allowed me to understand so much more of what he was thinking about before he could speak – insights that I never would have had if we hadn't used signing with him. On one occasion we went to the fair to see the animals ... which wasn't as exciting for Ethan as I'd first anticipated. I tried to engage him in signing about the animals, but he seemed quite uninterested. All of a sudden he became very excited and began making the sign for LIGHTS that he'd seen in the fairground. There were many other instances where the things we were showing him weren't the things he really wanted to see, but he was able to tell us – which was remarkable.

Baby-signing mum Georgia, Mytchett

Benefit 4:

Baby signing strengthens the bond between you and your baby

Obviously, where you have open lines of communication between people, you create deeper relationships. It is only natural, therefore, that when your baby is able to share his thoughts, feelings, desires and observations with you, your relationship with him is transformed.

Your baby will quickly learn that using sign language achieves far more than crying. Using signs helps you meet his needs more effectively and delights you when he describes something that interests him. Your child will be overjoyed when he initiates conversations – and you and other caregivers will be more attentive when he is able to express his feelings.

Understandably, being with your baby is more fun and rewarding when you can communicate with him. Interacting through sign lessens the number of negative exchanges and increases the opportunity for positive ones, resulting in more quality time. Reciprocal communication means a life that is shared rather than one that is separate. With sharing comes a stronger bond between you and your baby. As signs take hold, your child will also begin to look to you for information about the world and know that he can rely on you to give him that information – in a format that he can use.

But this stronger bond is not restricted to the relationship between you and your child. Closer ties are also formed with siblings, the extended family and those outside the realm of the family, such as friends and professional caregivers. When a baby learns to communicate, he becomes an active and integral part of the family and community, rather than just a passive observer waiting in the wings to emerge once he has learned how to speak.

Benefit 5:

Baby signing increases your baby's confidence

A healthy self-esteem will help your child navigate through life's challenges. It is attained when your child feels good about his capabilities and also has a strong sense that he is loved. Self-esteem develops better when both elements are present. For example, if your child is happy with his achievements but does not feel loved, he may experience low self-confidence. And if he feels loved but remains unconfident about his capabilities, he may also develop poor self-esteem.

Baby signing provides an additional tool to help establish and grow your baby's self-esteem. With every sign that your baby learns, he will experience a sense of accomplishment that will bolster his self-esteem. Communicating effectively with you will help him develop a high level of confidence and a strong 'can do' attitude. Your positive reaction to his communication will help him acknowledge his capability and help him feel that he is loved.

Research indicates that developing a healthy self-esteem early in life creates a solid, positive foundation for later years. It has already been proved that signing babies are more likely to grow up thinking well of themselves than non-signing babies. Signing babies tend to enjoy interacting with others and are comfortable in social situations more often than their non-signing peers. Signing babies are often not afraid to attempt new things. When challenges arise, signing babies are less likely to shy away from problems and more willing to search for solutions. Signing babies tend to have a belief in themselves and their own abilities, and they are more likely to grow up with an optimistic outlook on life than non-signing babies.

True Story

Sunny started to sign at 18 months. When she came to me one day and said, 'Tubby bye-byes' and signed GOODNIGHT, I almost fell off my chair. She'd used the sign in its proper context – albeit in Tellytubbies language – and she found it hilarious! She was so proud of herself when she saw my reaction that she repeated it over and over the next day! That same daughter is now ten years old, beautiful, intelligent and highly articulate. She's never had a problem with her speech – in fact, quite the opposite: most of the time we can't get a word in!

Baby-signing mum Paula, Worcester Park

Benefit 6:

Baby signing accelerates your baby's language development so that when speech begins, the content is more sophisticated

Some parents may worry that using sign language may interfere with their child's verbal language development. The fact is, a great deal of research shows the opposite is true. Not only does sign not limit speech development, it actually enhances communication to the point that children who sign tend to speak sooner and usually have more to say, as they begin to use words.

True Story

We had the most incredible experience with signs. By 18 months Toby was speaking and signing in three-word sentences. By the time he switched over to talking, he had a vocabulary of 75 signs. It wasn't that I was avidly teaching him signs. He was hooked on signing and wanted to know the sign for everything. Friends of ours were initially sceptical, but were bowled over at his ability to communicate. When he started speaking, it wasn't the usual 'Mama' and 'Dada' – it was, 'MORE BISCUITS, please, MUM!'

Baby-signing mum Rachel, East Dulwich

You should remember that for hearing babies sign language is not a substitute for speech. Signs used in conjunction with speech enhance language development. The two go hand in hand so that your baby can gradually begin to make the connection between the sign and the word and what you are talking about. Remember that when you are showing your baby a sign, the gesture must be done simultaneously with the word, until your baby associates the sign and the word with the event taking place or the object or action to which you are referring.

The greater the number of times you repeat a word to your child and combine it with a gesture, the quicker your child will understand the word and the sign's meaning, and that process leads to better comprehension of language. As the muscles that control speech mature, your child will transfer his manual language skills to his speech. The verbal and physical interaction between you and your baby makes the language learning process fun for both you and your baby. After all, you are spending time connecting with your child, which is one of the best ways to help his speech develop.

Research findings and my own observations indicate that signing children tend to show a stronger command of language than their non-signing peers when speech begins. Children who sign can often become leaders in their groups because they can affect their surroundings through communication. Of course, frustration is reduced with better communication, so more time is available for developmental activities such as painting, exploring and storytelling.

The regularity and the repetition of signing both assist in the development of your baby's scope of language. In simple terms, the more you speak and gesture to your child, the greater his vocabulary will be. Research shows that adding sign language to verbal communication after speech begins can boost your pre-school child's vocabulary, aid in spelling and usefully affect reading skills.

Before children learn to read themselves, signs offer a fun way to follow along as parents read. Children often ask for books that provide the opportunity to sign along. Seeing the word shape as the child makes the sign contributes to word identification. Signs, being expressive and dramatic, help to transform the reading process from being a passive to an interactive experience and cause your child's interest in books to escalate. Also, later in life when children are learning to read, they are forced to stop when they come up against a word they do not know. Equipped with a more extensive vocabulary they are less likely to stop on a word, which means that reading will, in turn, be less exasperating and more pleasurable.

Benefit 7:

Baby signing fuels intellectual development

Baby signing encourages intellectual development because babies are kept far busier, learning to link objects or actions with words and gestures. Their brains become a hive of activity as they become skilled at differentiating between a bird and a butterfly, or a hippo and an elephant, because anything less would not satisfy them.

True Story

I introduced signs to my twelve-month-old son Senol while reading bedtime stories with him. In time he began to sign BOOK, asking for stories during mealtimes. This kept him at the table longer and made mealtimes more fun. I really feel that signing made reading far more fascinating for Senol because it involved him exploring the pages, then signing and trying to say the word simultaneously. Senol is still passionate about reading, and we enjoy quiet bonding time together when I can sneak a cuddle without him noticing!

Baby-signing mum Sam, Esher

A behaviour that is often observed in signing children is play that is more advanced than in a non-signing child. Tending towards being better problem-solvers, signing children often approach playing with toys by investigating, pulling apart and seeing the toy's function at a more aggressive rate than non-signing children. Non-signing children tend to pick up the toy, examine it, but not to go to the same extent of trying to manipulate the toy in various ways, compared to children who sign.

Expert opinion

Acredolo and Goodwyn revisited the families in their original study when the children were seven and eight years old. The children who signed as babies had a mean IQ of 114 compared to the non-signing control group's mean IQ of 102. That's an average difference of 12 points!

I feel it is important to say that acquiring a higher IQ is not the reason to start signing with your baby. I am sure that in this age of cut-throat pre-school entrance exams, giving your baby an edge over others could seem an attractive incentive. However, the purpose of signing at a young age is not to create 'superior' babies. The emphasis is on nurturing the parent-child bond by bridging the communication gap during a short window in the developmental process. That, in itself, is remarkable.

Expert opinion: Signing stimulates brain activity

Studies on the brain have found that learning sign language uses more of the brain than learning a spoken language. When you learn how to speak a language, the information is absorbed and stored in the left side of the brain. However, when you learn sign language, the visual information is absorbed by the right side of the brain and then transported to the left side to be stored. In this way both the right and left sides of the brain are used, which has the result of increasing activity in the brain.

Let's not forget!

Some parents may wish to believe that signing will make their child run faster, jump higher, see through brick, and eventually sprout wings and fly! However, signs cannot effect any of those super-human feats. Signing is simply a wonderful way to communicate with your child much sooner than you would without it. What you do with that communication is up to you. For myself, my children and countless families, it has made all the difference in the world.

Sometimes what people fail to appreciate is that baby signing is, above all, very cute as well as tremendous fun for all of those participating in the rearing process. I received this wonderful letter from baby-signing mum Jenni, from Brighton, which I feel does a lot to encapsulate the heart of baby signing.

Most of the questions and quotes that I have come across with baby signing say that it relieves frustration – which it does – but what about the fun side of baby signing? Harvey was seven months old when he first signed MILK. At 16 months he signed his first full sentence. He had just had a long drink of milk and his tummy gurgled. 'What did you HEAR?' I signed to him. He thought long and hard, and then signed back to me, 'I HEARD a BIRD in my TUMMY.' What a fantastic insight into his personality! Harvey was so proud of himself for being able to communicate his idea. I will treasure this amusing experience forever.

How does signing fit into your baby's natural development?

Considering the benefits that baby signing can bring, it is not unreasonable to ask the question, 'Why?' – Why does it work? Why is it that babies seem not just willing but eager to sign? Why does it make them happier and less frustrated? Why does it accelerate language development and promote earlier speech?

These are all valid questions the answers to which are critical to your overall understanding of baby signing. Most important, you should know that baby signing is not a lucky accident that I and other experts accidentally stumbled across and that just happened to work. This chapter explains how signing and gestures are a fundamental part of your child's natural development and an essential part of growing up.

Language does not always involve speaking

People often equate their child's learning a language with learning to talk. Children who are deaf or hearing-impaired may never utter a single word – but their silence does not prevent them from learning and using language. Deaf people use an elaborate sign system, body movements, and facial expressions that contain all the critical features of language without spoken words.

Using speech is just one way to express language. Speech actually arrives comparatively late in your child's language development compared to her intellectual ability to understand the concept of language. Most children start using their first words around 12 months of age. Two- and three-word sentences emerge at around 18 to 21 months. What is the reason for this timetable? Most children are physically incapable of coordinating the numerous muscles in the mouth, tongue and larynx to produce speech until around the first year. Then, linking words together requires even more advanced levels of muscular coordination which requires further development.

However, just because your baby is not able to speak does not mean that she cannot understand the world around her. Parents often remain oblivious to their child's mammoth developmental achievements because there is no way to monitor those advances until speech begins. A young baby learns to identify her needs and wants, and experiments in various ways to express those needs and wants. When words are unavailable, every available method is tested. As your baby begins to realise that crying has limits when compared to the freely flowing ideas she is capable of creating, she either finds other ways of expressing herself or begins to learn the depths of her frustration. She seeks a method to remark about the objects, people and actions that impact on her life. You, as the parent, are there to guide her and show her the words (or signs) for these objects, people, and actions that influence her life. By the time she has mastered muscular skills to form verbal language, she is fairly far advanced in terms of understanding the need for language and how to use it.

Babies can produce language much earlier than they can speak

Learning to communicate

From the moment your child comes into the world, she wants to communicate. A parent's voice is familiar to the baby, and having heard it in the womb, she responds more to those voices than to any other sound. As I just mentioned, crying is your baby's principal means to get her needs met. Your baby will use different crying sounds to convey hunger, fear, pain or boredom. She uses whatever means she has available to her to communicate, including smiling, watching your face, giggling and reaching. She attempts to produce speech-like sounds long before clear spoken words emerge. Her babbling patterns will develop from what seem like random sounds to conversational-style rhythms. You will notice that she will babble and then offer a pause for your response – a similar send-and-respond rhythm exhibited by adults. This signifies that she is developing an understanding of how two-way communication works.

Connecting signs or words with meanings

At around four months old, your baby begins to focus, to be attracted to movement, and is able to recall objects and sounds. During the next few months her scope expands. She starts making sense of the noise and activity around her. She is drawn to objects that interest her, especially anything that is brightly coloured, that has sound, that has an interesting shape or that moves. She begins to recognise routine patterns that emerge in daily events and to notice the signs and words that accompany those events.

Your baby begins to understand the connection between the events and the language, whether that language is expressed in words or signs. She begins to register that certain events tend to happen together, such as when she screams and Mummy comes running, or when Mummy approaches her with a bottle and feeding time begins. Her ability to recognise a link between two events, or a sign/word and an event, is a milestone in her language development.

Your baby begins to understand the meanings of words and signs at around her sixth or seventh month. She begins to grasp the connection between words or signs and what those words or signs represent. For example, she learns that the word/sign 'TEDDY' means the furry bear that she takes to bed. At this stage in her development she possesses the ability to communicate but is still constrained by her inability to articulate words clearly.

How her motor skills support gestures or signs

While her mental development is progressing she is also making strides in her physical development. By the time she is six to eight months old, her motor skills have developed sufficiently to allow her to hold on to objects and move them around with a fair degree of control.

Once she understands the relationship between words and signs and the things those words and signs represent, she can begin to construct language. Because she has more control over her hands than her voice, she can use her hands to form signs before she can use her voice to clearly say words.

Her first attempts at making the signs may be malformed, as her first attempts to pronounce words are bound to be. Baby babbling occurs in both manual and verbal forms. Babies will babble with their hands prior to forming more exact signs. She will continue to attempt to make the signs and pronounce the words until she gets the appropriate response or sees and hears the correct version enough times to realise her version is not the same as the parent's.

At around eight months your baby is still limited in her verbal abilities and has great difficulty pronouncing words. However, her manual dexterity has now developed to the extent that she is able to start mimicking your gestures, and she naturally gravitates towards using signs rather than words. Her ability to learn to use signs to communicate is rapid. She can now hold her arms up or point to something she desires, even though she is unable to say, 'Please pick me up,' or 'I want that.'

By the age of 12 months, your child begins to 'take off' in terms of understanding and using language. Her first words may start to appear but her motor skills are advanced enough to enable her to make a large number of signs and develop a considerable vocabulary within a very short time. At 16 months her vocal chords are now fully formed, but she is still able only to use single words. On the other hand, she is dexterous enough to be using a great number of signs. By 18 to 21 months old she has started to say two- and three-word sentences. And by two years old she is talking the hind leg off a donkey, using increasingly complex sentences and asking more elaborate questions. Now her motor skills are supporting the rapid and fluid movement of her signing alongside her words.

How bright your little spark really is!

Obviously, every baby progresses at her own particular and personal rate. The following information nonetheless offers an approximate timetable of your baby's capabilities.

- At around four months old she can recall objects and sounds.

- At six to seven months she can understand the general meanings of words and begins to babble.

- At eight months she can start mimicking gestures and actions and may well have made her first few signs.

- At 12 months her first word may well have already appeared. Her motor skills are advanced and she can make a large number of signs. Many babies can form short signed sentences.

- At 16 months her vocal chords are now fully formed but she is still using single words. Her motor skills support an expanding vocabulary, and most babies are combining signs to form short sentences.

- Between 18 and 21 months old she can say two- and three-word sentences. Some signs are dropped as words take their place.

- At 24 months she is using increasingly complex sentences and asking more elaborate questions. Her motor skills support the rapid and fluid movement of her signing alongside her words.

Why signs work so well

It has been known for years among hearing parents of deaf children and deaf parents of hearing children that babies learn to communicate through sign language much earlier than they can learn to speak. Signs have therefore proved extremely helpful both to infants who had to use them of necessity and to others for whom the signs have additionally been a springboard to verbal communication.

It is clear why babies themselves welcome the use of signs over words during their first two years. Babies can sign before they can speak.

Sign language takes a child's natural tendency to gesture and builds upon it by apportioning a systematic and consistent code to the movements. It encourages, extends, and advances what she is naturally doing already. It takes advantage of the hand skills that are developed, rather than waiting another year for the speech mechanism to mature. Gestures allow a more effective and sophisticated way to communicate.

What happens when your baby learns signs

Consider the process your child goes through when she learns to say 'milk'. The sound 'milk' has no inherent meaning, but your baby quickly learns to associate that word with the warm liquid substance she gets when she is hungry. In this way the sound of the word 'milk' becomes a reference for food, and you have to say it to her over and over again, in context, until she finally connects the sound to the object.

Learning to sign is exactly the same process. If you repeatedly use the sign for MILK in context, your baby will eventually come to understand its reference to milk. Her first revelation arises when she discovers the connection between her making the sign and your reaction to her sign. As she gets results, her sign usage is reinforced and her communication journey begins.

Her ability to connect signs with meaning develops step by step. Initial attempts to form signs may be a bit crude, but she will persist until she gains an acceptable level of accuracy. The more signs she sees, the more she will use. The more signs she uses, the more resourceful she will become, as she uses signs to navigate her way through life. These are her first real steps to empowerment!

The Baby Signing process

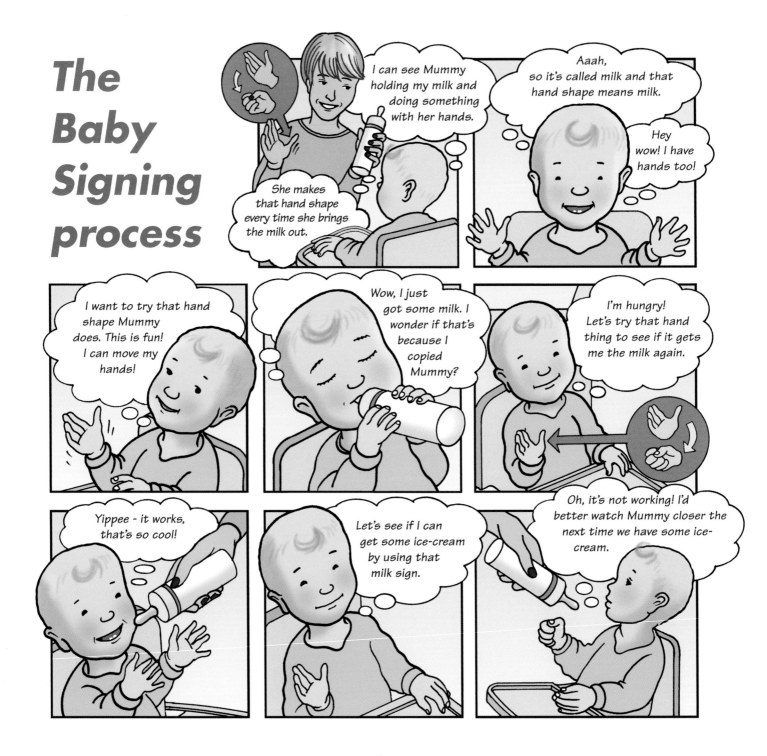

Moving from signing to speaking

It is certainly true that the ability to speak arrives shortly after the ability to sign. However, the number of signs your baby is able to make at an early age dramatically exceeds the number of words she can enunciate clearly enough to be understood. Signs are so practical and useful during the early stages of communication that your baby will rely on them to satisfy her needs. As she begins to comprehend more about her world, she will be inspired to comment at greater length about the things she understands beyond her basic needs. An instinctive desire to speak emerges. As she learns to speak, the signs become more and more unnecessary. The journey from signs to speech begins.

At around 12 months of age, many children attempt to say more and more words. Children begin saying words for the signs they know, and if misunderstood, use the signs for backup. Often, children who have an average sign vocabulary by the first year – around 20 to 50 signs – start creating short, signed sentences from around the age of 14 to 17 months. I see many babies able to sign 100 signs by their fourteenth month. Talking in short sentences, made up of nouns and verbs, seems to take off in the second year. By the age of 18 months a signing child may well have a vocabulary of 300 words and/or signs compared to his non-signing peers' average of between ten and 50 words.

True Story

We started signing with Leahlahni when she was nine months old. At 18 months I listed all the words she could say and sign, and it came to over 80, while many of her peers hardly said a word.

Now, at almost 22 months, she rarely signs but will sign if, for example, her mouth is full or we are a distance from each other. She speaks exceptionally well, so that even strangers can tell what she is saying, and uses four- or five-word sentences. Signing is just a game. We sign the word to Leahlahni and Leahlahni will say the word back to us.

We think it has been absolutely brilliant. Our families were dubious about us doing this with our daughter, and work colleagues thought it would hinder her speech, but in actual fact it has greatly enhanced her language skills. I'd recommend it to any new mums.

Baby signing Dad, Finn from Littlehampton

CHAPTER FOUR

True Story

My youngest daughter, at toddler group, likes the fact that while she's at one end of the room where the biscuits and juice are, and I'm at the other end of the room, she can sign that she wants MORE BISCUITS or MORE JUICE without having to come and get me. She waits until she's caught my eye and signs to me, and has done so since she was 14 months old. There's another signing mum at the group and Sophie knows that if she's there, she can sign to this other lady and she'll get a biscuit or juice as well. This would never have been possible if we'd decided to invent our own signs.

Baby-signing mum Lucie, Lincolnshire

Standardised signs are highly beneficial in classrooms because they offer consistency across childcare and educational settings. BSL is already being used in many schools and is increasingly becoming a part of the normal curriculum.

Expert opinion

Yvonne Lavelle, Director of Eviecare Childcare Consultants in Glasgow, Scotland, says that

'We advocate the use of standardised signs throughout the childcare system. It is very important to show the same signs to babies to avoid confusion at a later stage of development. Nurseries and nannies are progressively using Joseph Garcia's programme throughout their normal curriculum. It is a fantastic way of communicating and a step into the future for our children.'

In today's society, special needs children are integrated wherever possible into society. Establishing a connection, via a standardised sign system, between children who are developing traditionally and those with learning difficulties such as cerebral palsy, Down's Syndrome and autism is a massive leap forward for our children. It is unquestionable that sharing this common connection would allow students with disabilities to feel more at ease with other children.

> **True Story**
>
> Both my children have befriended a little boy with Down's syndrome who uses signing, and when Henry comes over to play, there's no problem with communication. I know Henry really appreciates this. It would have been a terrible loss if this hadn't been possible.
>
> Emma of Babysigners, Hove

Advantage number 2:

It is a recognised second language that you can use for the rest of your life

If you use a standardised language, the system of signs you learn will be valuable once your child learns to speak. With the increase in sign language programmes from pre-school to college level emerging in the educational world, early exposure to signing gives your child a start on a valuable second language. He can continue to use this language as he gets older and, indeed, for the rest of his life. The benefit of learning a second language would of course extend to you, the parent, and to any other family members who learn it along with you.

> **Expert opinion**
>
> Dr Marilyn Daniels – who has more than ten years' experience researching hearing babies and children in the USA and in the UK – advocates the use of standardised over home-made signs.
>
> 'Not only does sign language empower children when they are very young, but if the signs are standardised, it plants the seeds for continued learning of signing. These children receive a jump-start on mastering a valuable second language skill when they are older.'

Advantage number 3:

Signs are easy to learn and easy to understand

As a busy parent in the twenty-first century, you may well feel daunted at the prospect of learning another whole language. But the great news is that you do not have to. Successfully communicating with your baby does not require fluency in a sign language like BSL. All you need are a few signs to start off with and, when you feel comfortable with these, just add a few more.

Many BSL signs are iconic – which means that they look like the action or object to which they refer. For example, the WASH FACE sign is just pretending to wash your face, and the BRUSH TEETH sign mimics the movements of brushing your teeth. Simple! That means that you and your baby will have little problem recognising and remembering what many signs stand for. This is in stark contrast to words in which the sound of the word has no connection to the object, or action, it represents.

Advantage number 4:

You can never forget signs

One potential frustration for parents who are creating their own sign system is the need not only to create unique signs but to memorise them as well. Imagine showing your baby a sign – then forgetting it a few days later. And how would you feel if your baby signed back to you and you could not remember what that sign meant? With a standardised sign language you would have books, charts and other resources at your disposal making this situation unlikely to occur.

Advantage number 5:

Signs don't interfere with speech

When inventing signs, some parents decide to make up a sign for their baby that involves blowing, sniffing or some other movement involving the mouth. This becomes problematic when their child learns to talk, because now it is impossible for him to speak and sign simultaneously. It is also impossible for the parent to sign and speak simultaneously, which is problematic because the child's need to understand the relationship between signed and spoken words is critical. Standardised signs use positioning hands and animated facial expressions, but never cause interference with speech.

The Golden Rules of baby signing

In this chapter I hope to give you a map for your exciting journey through early communication. I am sure you are eager to get started with the practical part of signing. I will provide you with easy-to-follow baby-signing guidelines and introduce you to the seven Golden Rules of baby signing.

The seven Golden Rules of baby signing

1   Use signs that are relevant to your baby's needs and interests.
2   Use facial expressions and sign in your baby's sight line.
3   Repetition is the key to success.
4   Say the word as you sign.
5   Show your baby the object as you sign and always sign correctly.
6   Be patient – every child is different and learning takes time!
7   Be responsive to your baby's signs and keep it FUN!

Start signing with your baby when she starts to focus – but it is never too late to start

Before I go a little deeper into the seven Golden Rules, I would like to take a closer look at getting started.

There is no 'right age' to begin signing. If you choose to, you can begin learning and showing the signs to your baby from birth. However, keep in mind that you are unlikely to see any results until she is between eight and ten months old. Up until then, your baby is still in the process of developing her cognitive skills, memory, and dexterity in order to distinguish, remember, and produce the signs.

I recommend that you introduce signs to her after her fourth month when she is beginning to focus. It is quite easy to tell when she is ready to learn them – her eyes will start connecting with yours.

If you prefer to wait till later on in her life, even if she is already speaking but has a limited vocabulary, she will still benefit from using signs to communicate her needs. Babies with 50 to 100 words in their vocabularies continue to find some words too difficult to say, like 'elephant' or 'hippopotamus'. In situations such as these, signing would therefore be valuable.

A good place to start would be MILK and MORE

The number of signs that you introduce to your baby depends entirely on you. You can start with as few or as many as you wish. Never restrict the number of signs you show your baby any more than you would worry about overloading her with the number of words you say. Your baby's ability to learn signs is limitless, and she will merely focus on those she finds valuable in her world. No matter how enthused you are, she will begin using the signs she wants when she is ready. What you are providing, by showing her a lot of signs, is a broader menu to choose from as language begins to take hold.

Milk

MILK and MORE

I recommend starting with MILK and MORE because these are the most commonly used words throughout the day and you will find many opportunities to use them. Use the MILK sign when your baby is breast-feeding or bottle-feeding. To make the sign for MILK, open and close your fist several times, as the illustration shows. Make the sign away from your chest if it is a bottle and over your chest if it is breast milk, to help differentiate the two. Make this sign *before*, *during* and *after* you nurse or feed her. You'll know when your baby recognises MILK because she will show eagerness when you make the sign.

If MILK is the first sign she learns, you may find that she uses it to mean almost everything. Remember, she made a gesture and got a response, so she will experiment to see what other results she can obtain from you by making that same gesture. When she becomes aware that different signs are required to get different things, she will be on the lookout to learn other signs that you show her.

True Story

I think signing's wonderful. At 13 months Tessa was still nursing, and during one early morning feed when we were both very bleary-eyed, she looked up at me and signed MILK ALL GONE. We switched sides and were both happy – Tessa because she had more milk, and I because I was glowing with pride.

Baby-signing mum Kate, Luton

More

MORE is another essential sign that many babies produce first. When your child has finished a portion of food, say and sign, 'MORE?' and give her more food. MORE becomes a useful sign to enable her to request more food, more stories, more play, more cuddles, more anything.

Every time you use the word 'more', show your baby the MORE sign. Always use the correct sign, repeat it often, and emphasise the word with the sign. This process will help your baby clearly see and hear the connection between the word/sign and the thing that is taking place. 'Do you want some MORE? You'd like some MORE, would you? OK – let's get you some MORE.' A questioning look and tone will help her understand what you are asking.

> ### True Story
>
>
>
> We started signing MORE and MILK to Jess when she was nine months old, and two months later she began making them. I noticed that she'd always look at our hands when we spoke to her. She made the sign for MILK every time she saw us heating her milk on the stove at night – and MORE was a great success because of the grapes we used to encourage her to make it!
>
> Baby-signing mum Julie, South Yorkshire

Adding more signs

As you feel at ease with your first few signs, then start adding more signs. There is no need to wait until your baby has started signing back to you. Just keep adding as many signs as you wish, bearing in mind that the more signs you present, the more signs she will have at her disposal.

The wealth of signs that you'll find in Part II will help you in this process. These signs are grouped according to the specific activities that make up your daily routine – for example, changing her nappy, feeding her, dressing or bathing her. By learning five to ten signs for each routine, you could quickly learn 50 to 100 signs with little effort.

Golden Rule number 1:

Use signs that are relevant to your baby's needs and interests

When learning new signs, take your cue from your baby. Does she love the cat? Does she adore spending time with her granny? What are her favourite toys? What animals fascinate her when you're reading a book together? By watching her attentively, you will soon discover which words/signs she is most interested in learning.

Some other popular first signs

MUMMY, DADDY, GRANNY, GRANDPA, BABY

CAT, DOG, BIRD

SHOE, BOOK

WHERE?

FINISHED, ALL GONE

Interestingly, my daughter Alaina picked up on FINISHED to indicate that she had had enough of something. When we read a book that contained a character that frightened her, she would sign FINISHED to mean that she wanted to change books! On one occasion our aeroplane was grounded on the tarmac for four long hours, due to security issues. After pacing the aisles several times and seeing all that she needed to see, Alaina signed FINISHED, implying that she was ready to go home. The remaining three hours and 40 minutes was an experience I would wish on no one!

Golden Rule number 2:

Use facial expressions and sign in your baby's sightline

As much as 75 per cent of language is non-verbal. This means that as humans we rely heavily on facial expression, body posture, movement and eye contact to convey and receive meaning. When you sign with your baby, exaggerate your facial expressions and body language as much as possible, and don't be shy! Being animated will delight your child and aid her in her understanding of what you are trying to communicate.

For example, when you make the SCARED sign, make your whole body tremble and look frightened. Or when you make the sign for HAPPY, let your expression tell the story. Using expressive vocal tones for emphasis when you are articulating the words will also help your baby understand and learn language.

There is a visual 'line of sight' between you and your child. Look into her eyes as you are signing, and when appropriate, keep the sign close to your face. This will greatly improve your chances of success. A good time to introduce a sign is when her gaze meets yours.

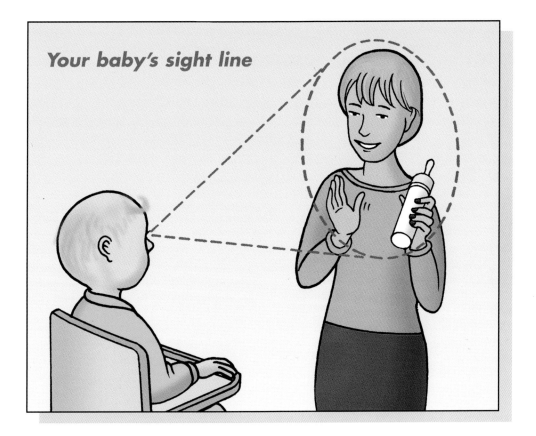

Your baby's sight line

Golden Rule number 3:

Repetition is the key to success

Language development requires repeated exposure to the language. If you want your child to talk, you will have to talk to her as much as possible. It is exactly the same with the signing process. If you want your child to sign, you will have to repeatedly, and consistently, sign to her.

Children learn best through repetition, which is one of the most important principles of sign language. Give your child maximum exposure to signs, incorporating them during routine events. Give her descriptive accounts during these daily rituals, adding signs for interesting objects. Sing to her and add the signs during songs. Read to her and use signs for objects or animals. Use colourful images in books and magazines to stimulate interest. Speak slowly and clearly in short sentences.

It is only through repeated exposure to signs that your baby will observe a sign, decipher its meaning, analyse the context and conclude that there is a relationship between the sign/word and the event. It is only through constant repetition that she will understand the power that comes with communication and be able to begin producing the signs herself.

Try to develop consistent signing habits. You could post reminders of the signs, grouped by topic, around the house for easy reference. Use the signs at every opportunity. Create opportunities for her to use the signs. Continue to make the signs even after she has begun signing. Never stop using the signs she already knows. Make the signs even if she is not watching you.

The one-way communication from you to your baby is as important as the two-way communication between the two of you. The signs you show her will help your child understand the world, clarify events, and let her know what is coming next. Do not expect your baby to use all the signs you show her. Sometimes your signs will be intended to prepare her for what is coming next or to give a command, or will be addressing a parenting issue and not necessarily be a sign that she will want to use herself, like the sign WAIT or DON'T TOUCH.

Inform members in both your immediate and extended families, caregivers, and friends that you are signing with your baby, and encourage them to participate. Your baby will learn much faster if she is observing the same signs being used by Grandpa, Grandma, siblings, and the babysitter. Involving core family members will lessen the frustration she may feel when she attempts to communicate with others she cares about and they do not know what she is trying to say. It also offers brothers, sisters, cousins, and grandparents an opportunity to bond with the baby, and will make them feel included.

The fastest way to jump-start your baby into communicating is to have her interact with her older brother or sister. Studies show that given equal time, an older child can teach a younger child faster than an adult could teach the same child.

True Story

I started signing with my three-year-old daughter at the same time as I introduced signs to my eight-month-old son. Amy learned the signs much more quickly than I did. She started signing to her baby brother, and within a couple of months they were communicating back and forth. I often had to ask her the meaning of a sign Oliver was using, because they always remembered more signs than I did! Oliver would tell me if Amy didn't translate his signs correctly. By the time Oliver was a year old, they were both using complete sentences. Watching them 'converse' brought tears to my eyes more times than I can remember.

Baby-signing mum Hayley, Hendon

Golden Rule number 4:

Say the word as you sign

Generally, always reinforce the sign with the word so that your baby can clearly hear and see the connection between the two. For example, when you ask her, 'Would you like a drink?' combine the sign for DRINK with the question: 'Would you like a DRINK?'

There are a couple of exceptions to this – namely, when you are toilet training or disciplining your child and do not wish to embarrass her in public. Also, once your baby firmly understands a sign and you are having a serene moment, you may wish to sign something and maintain the quiet, knowing that she will understand with or without saying the word.

Golden Rule number 5:

Show your baby the object as you sign and always sign correctly

Make sure that you sign in context at the appropriate time, or your baby will not have the slightest clue what you are trying to communicate! For example, sign CHANGE just before changing your baby's nappy, UP as you pick her up, BATH as you are about to bath her, or HUG before hugging her. Showing her the signs in context will help her understand the association between the signs/words you make and her experiences.

Similarly, using one sign in a variety of appropriate contexts will show your baby how words/signs can be used in different situations and help her to develop and understand language. For example, if you sign and say FINISHED after you have put on her nappy, when you have put on her clothes, or when you have completed the story you were reading, she will quickly absorb its meaning and will begin using FINISHED in various situations.

Sign only for things that are in the sight of your child. If she is younger than two, she sees the world in concrete terms and is not yet able to grasp abstract concepts. When you are making the signs for objects, try to point directly at them, or even touch them. For example, when you sign for BALL, point and touch the ball, or when making the PAIN sign, touch the relevant body part to indicate that she has just hurt herself. This will greatly assist in clarifying exactly what you mean.

When your baby decides that she is ready to start communicating with you, she will be eager to start experimenting. As I mentioned earlier, she will go through a stage of babbling with her hands, trying to replicate the signs that she observes. This is exactly the same process she goes through when she babbles with her mouth, mimicking the sounds she hears around her.

It is crucial that you make the signs correctly, even if your child does not. Don't adapt to your baby's version. Rather, show her how to make a sign. For example, if your daughter is having a difficult time making the sign for 'drink', carry her to the fridge and take out some orange juice. Then say to her, 'There you go, Tina – there's something to drink.' As you say 'drink', make the sign by holding your hand up to your lips in the shape of a cup. Then, gently take your child's hand, and while saying 'drink', place her hand to her mouth to sign DRINK. Turn it into a game. If she is reluctant to participate, do not force her. She will get better at replicating the signs as her dexterity improves, just as her words become more clearly pronounced when her speech mechanism matures.

In the meantime, show her version to the rest of the family so that they understand what she is trying to sign. I guarantee that when her little fingers start perfecting the signs, she will swell with pride and melt your heart!

Golden Rule number 6:

Be patient – every child is different and learning takes time!

As parents, we love to see results. A child's first step, first words, or first anything are great moments of achievement and confirm to us that our child is developing.

In my work with families I am often approached by parents concerned that their baby has not produced a sign after being exposed to them for two or three months. I have heard some parents remark, 'I used signs for several weeks, but my child didn't catch on, so we gave up!' That is similar to saying, 'We talked for several weeks but my child didn't say anything, so the family stopped talking!'

Having to wait three to five months before your baby signs back to you may occasionally test your patience. Yet if you stop to consider all the activity – the observing, processing, and learning – that takes place in her brain in order to produce language, such a short period seems quite remarkable.

Usually babies start signing between eight and 14 months if you, the parent, start signing around the seventh month. However, exactly when your child begins to sign will depend on a wide range of factors:

Your baby's age – the younger she is when you start signing, the longer it will take for her first signs to appear.

How developed her related skills are (i.e. memory, dexterity, cognition) – the more developed she is, the sooner she will begin to produce signs.

How frequently you, and other caregivers, show the signs to her – the more consistent you and other caregivers are, on a daily basis, the sooner she will sign.

How interested she is in communicating – she may be more interested in playing with her toys than in using signing to communicate with you!

Children navigate themselves through learning in different ways. Some pick up on the signs quickly and begin using them immediately. Others watch and wait until the need becomes great enough to experiment. Then all of a sudden a baby will gush forth with signs and words. Yet others express their understanding of language a little at a time and tend to observe more closely before signing back.

Some children learn more than 200 signs before, and during, the transition to speech. Others use only a dozen signs before speech begins. When you consider the environment and external human influences, along with the individual learning issues, comparing children before they are two years old is absolutely fruitless. It is important to remember that your baby has her own unique development schedule and will decide when she needs language in order to communicate with you.

True Story

I signed to Henry from when he was six months old, but didn't see a single sign from him until he was 13 months old. After that it was like a torrential outpouring of signs, one after the other, until he had accumulated a vocabulary of more than 50 signs. These he used consistently, until his speech 'explosion' at the age of 22 months.

Baby-signing mum Nadia, North London

How long it takes your child to sign, and the number of signs she expresses, should always be secondary to the issue of your personal relationship. Patience is a crucial ingredient in the baby-signing process. Showing impatience, disappointment and frustration will breed uncertainty, anxiety, and discouragement in your child. Committing to the baby-signing adventure takes time and courage, and if your commitment is diluted, the results could be significantly diminished. Maintaining a sense of trust in both the process and your abilities will sooner or later result in the incredible experience of a glorious communication between you and your child.

CHAPTER FIVE

She signs!

The feeling of exhilaration that parents experience when they see their baby's first sign is indescribable – much the same as if their baby has uttered her first word or taken her first step.

Tessa signs 'aeroplane'

 True Story

When my son Bryn was seven months old, I introduced him to Joseph Garcia's signing programme. I started him off with MILK, EAT and MORE, using them at every opportunity, and about six weeks later I noticed that he was registering exactly what I was saying to him. At about nine months old, he had just finished his bowl of mashed potato when he looked over and signed MORE. I nearly jumped out of my skin with delight.

Baby-signing dad Thomas, Birmingham

Part II

Putting baby signing into action

Signs of life

Creating real magic

As you already know, your baby possesses an extraordinary inclination towards communication and interaction from the moment he is born. He is highly attuned to the sounds and movements within his environment and, depending upon the nature of that environment, is able to make advances early in his life.

Clear communication is one of the greatest gifts you could ever hope to give your baby. Speaking slowly and clearly during the first few months of your baby's life has invaluable benefits – perhaps the greatest being that it strengthens the parent-child bond and is critical to your child's language development.

What about when you add signs to your speech? Adding signs goes even further to signalling your responsiveness and love for him. Now, not only are you showing him attention with words but you are also demonstrating your devotion through gestures. It is a symbol of your total engagement with, and availability to, your child. It is your acknowledgement that he is a real and unique person who has an abundance to learn and contribute.

When you combine words and signs into daily routines, you set the scene for the creation of real magic. No one knows more than you do the power that routines and rituals have in babies' lives. Babies feel security in the rhythm and order that routine brings. Infants are soothed by the regularity and reliability that comes from routine.

Routines are, in essence, the perfect environment in which to introduce something new to your child.

Using this section

As a father of three, I know how excruciatingly difficult it is to set aside any time in a busy schedule for learning new things. One of my greatest motivations for designing my Complete Guide to Baby Signing was to develop a signing system that suited the diary of the most overworked parent.

One great advantage of my new programme is that it will fit into any schedule. Rather than trying to set aside specific times to learn with your baby, you can merely integrate the signs into your already well-established routines.

Another advantage is that all the signs have been grouped together according to those routines, as they occur throughout your day. All you have to do is open up the Activities section of this book at the routine you happen to be engaged in at the time (for example, Changing your baby's nappy, Getting dressed or Bedtime). For each one you will find six recommended signs. Learn, practise and get comfortable with these signs. Then begin to use the signs that suit the particular needs of your baby.

An example

Let me give you an example. You are about to change your baby's nappy. Turn to Changing your baby's nappy in the Activities section. Choose two or three signs, such as WET, CHANGE and FINISHED. Examine and practise the hand shape, the position, and the movement of each sign.

When you have your child's attention, start showing him each sign. Use each sign before, during and/or immediately after the event as you talk about it. Say the words as they normally feature in your sentence, and sign as you say the key words, 'Are you WET? Let's CHANGE your nappy. I'm all FINISHED.' Always make the sign close to your face, in the sight line between you and your child.

Have no fear!

If this sounds a bit daunting at first, there is no need to worry. Just go at your own pace and you will be amazed at your capacity to learn 30 to 50 signs in a fairly short time.

Have no fear about overwhelming your child with too many signs. Would you limit the number of words you spoke to him in a day? No! Well then, there is no need to limit the number of signs you use. Your little child's mind absorbs information just as a sponge absorbs water. Like words, the more signs you expose him to, the more he will learn. Then as he learns to control his hands and begins to understand language, the more signs he will have at his fingertips for use later.

Additional signs

In every section, you will find up to six additional signs. I suggest that you familiarise yourself with the recommended signs first, and then move on to the additional ones.

Crossing over

Occasionally, you will find that I have included one sign in several different routines. For example, the sign FINISHED has many uses. I have done this so that your child can see this sign used in different situations – for instance, when he has finished his book, when he has finished eating or when his mother has finished changing his nappy.

Caregiver signs

Some of the signs are caregiver signs. Although the caregiver signs are not used by your baby, these signs let your baby know what is happening or about to happen. However, these signs are important because they help to reinforce the meaning of the expression to your baby. The DON'T TOUCH sign is one example of this.

Above all, have fun!

The main aim of my programme is for you to have fun! You are not 'teaching' signs to your baby: you are simply adding signs to your daily speech in a fun way. You are exposing your baby to a positive learning environment in which he is eager to participate. Your attitude when learning and making the signs will make all the difference. The more fun you have and the more playful your attitude is, the more your child will learn. It is that simple. I have repeatedly heard from countless parents that signing is one of the most extraordinary experiences they shared with their babies.

Enjoy, and good luck!

Good morning, Sunshine!

- When you go into your baby's room, say and sign, 'Are you AWAKE?' (with an inquisitive expression) or 'WAKE UP, darling!'

- If your baby has a doll or a stuffed animal, play *waking up the doll* by signing and saying, 'WAKE UP!' as you 'awaken' the doll or animal from its 'slumber'.

- The first place your baby wants to be in the morning is in your arms. This is the time to introduce the sign for UP. Say and sign, 'Do you want to come UP?', using an enquiring expression. Then pick him up and say, 'Up you come!'

- Say and sign, 'It's time to GET READY' just before and while you are getting him ready.

- When it is time to wash his face and brush his teeth, prepare him for each activity by saying the words and showing him the sign. 'Let's WASH your FACE.' 'Now let's BRUSH your TEETH.' The *hygiene* signs such as WASH FACE, BRUSH TEETH and BRUSH HAIR are simply miming actions. The sign for WASH FACE is making the motion to wash your face. Use your finger as the brush to brush your teeth, or all fingers to brush your hair, and so on.

- Use the TOILET sign when your child is relieving himself. You can also use TOILET when he is watching you or sees other children using the toilet. In time, he will learn to let you know when he needs to 'go'.

- Say and sign 'HUG' before you give your child a cuddle.

- Take your baby to the window, then sign and say, 'LOOK!' Describe what you see outside. If it is raining, sign RAIN and say, 'It's raining!' Is it cold or hot? Say and sign, 'It's COLD!' or 'It's HOT!', using lots of body language and facial expression.

- Before you move from one place to another you can say and sign, 'Let's GO', making the sign in the direction you are going.

+ Additional signs

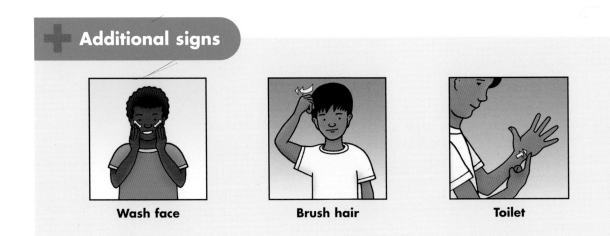

Wash face　　　**Brush hair**　　　**Toilet**

Wake up/awake

Up!

Get ready

Hug

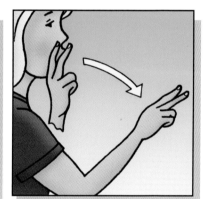

Look!

Let's go!

Rain

Cold

Hot

45

Nappy times!

- When it is time to change your baby's nappy, first get his attention. Then make the CHANGE sign in his sight line as you say, 'Darling, it's time to change your nappy.'

- Lay him on his back and, as you start changing him, say and sign, 'CHANGE', and then change him.

- When you have completed the process, look into your baby's eyes, and say and sign, 'FINISHED'.

- Use the signs CHANGE and FINISHED consistently every time you change him.

- CHANGE is a caregiver sign that many babies do not make until their second year. But it is useful because it provides a clue to what is about to happen to your child. Once he is walking and his sight-line area broadens, you can begin signing NAPPY and CHANGE together. Then, if you wish, eventually drop CHANGE or NAPPY. This is because NAPPY carries the same meaning as CHANGE, and each sign can be used on its own to represent the entire process.

- Eventually, you can say and sign 'NAPPY' as you reach for a new nappy to help your baby learn that 'nappy' is the object and 'change' the activity.

- When you feel you are ready, add new signs like DIRTY, WET, CLEAN and CREAM to your signing repertoire.

- Say and sign, 'WET' or 'DIRTY' as soon as you discover the state of your child's nappy. Using each sign for the appropriate purpose will reinforce the difference between his bladder and bowel movements.

- When the room fills with the aroma of nappy filler, you could say and sign, 'SMELLY!' Make sure your face depicts a playful rather than a disgusted expression, or your child may start to believe that his smells are shameful.

- If the wipes are a little cold, say and sign, 'COLD' just before you wipe his bottom clean.

- When you are finished cleaning him, sign DRY just before you sign FINISHED. Say, '[Your baby's name] is DRY now. That means we are FINISHED!'

+ Additional signs

Nappy

Smelly

Cold

Change

Finished

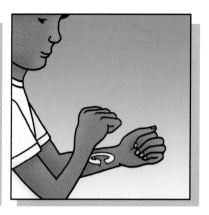

Dirty

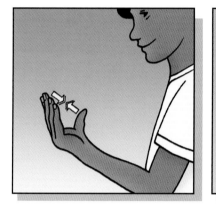

Wet

Clean

Cream

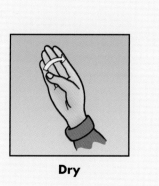

Dry

ACTIVITIES

Dressed for success!

- When your child is ready to get dressed in the morning, sign CLOTHES. The CLOTHES sign represents the entire dressing process. Make the entire process fun - sort of like a mime game. First, you mime the action - for instance, putting on a shirt. Then repeat the action and put on your baby's shirt.

- SOCKS and SHOES are some of the first articles of clothing your child notices. You can add these two signs just before and while you are putting his socks and shoes on him.

- Sign HAT as you put his hat on his head.

- As he begins to dress himself, you can add the HELP sign. If you see him struggling, say and sign, 'Would you like some HELP?'

- Say and sign, 'It's time to GET READY' just before you are getting him ready.

- Finish dressing your child, then sign and say, 'All FINISHED!'

- Most signs for getting dressed are mimed signs that resemble the action - for example, pretending to put on your trousers, one leg at a time, or placing an imaginary shirt over your head and extending each arm.

- When putting on warm clothes, you can make the sign COLD, saying, 'It's COLD outside.'

- You can put your baby's hat and coat on him, saying and signing, 'Your HAT and COAT will keep you WARM.'

- A great sign to introduce is the WHERE? sign. Any time you are looking for them, say and sign, 'WHERE are your SHOES?', 'WHERE is your HAT?'. Acting out the search process will help your child understand the meaning of 'where?'.

- Do not forget to make the signs in your baby's sight line!

+ Additional signs

Get ready

Finished

Cold

Clothes/get dressed

Hat

Coat

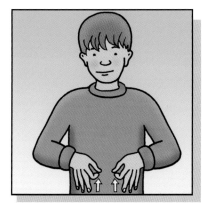

Sock/s

Shoe/s

Help

Warm

Where?

ACTIVITIES

Let's eat!

- 'Milk' is one of the most important and most frequently reoccurring activities for your baby, and is an ideal sign to start with.

- Make the MILK sign over your breast when you are referring to breast-feeding, and away from your body when you are referring to bottled milk.

- Say and make the sign 'MILK' just before and while you are feeding your baby.

- As he begins to eat solid food, you can start using the sign EAT. Just before mealtime, say and sign, 'EAT' when you have your child's attention. That alerts him to what is about to happen.

- You can use the words EAT and FOOD interchangeably.

- MORE is one of the most useful signs. When your child has finished a portion of food, say and sign, 'Would you like some MORE?' with a questioning look. Then give him a little

more. The more you repeat this, the more familiar your baby will become with the concept, and the sooner he will start to use it.

- Sign and say, 'Have you FINISHED? Yes - well done, darling: you have FINISHED!'

- When there is no more food left, the sign ALL GONE can be added.

- When your child is old enough to drink from a cup, you can use the sign DRINK to mean the object (e.g. juice) or the action. Sign and say, 'Do you want a DRINK?', using an inquisitive expression.

- The sign FULL is useful to show enough food has been eaten. This sign can be a playful one used after a big meal.

- You can use WARM, HOT and COLD to describe the food's temperature.

+ Additional signs

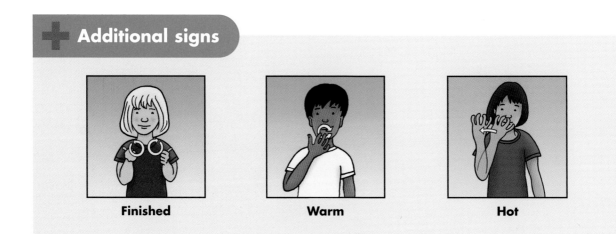

Finished   **Warm**   **Hot**

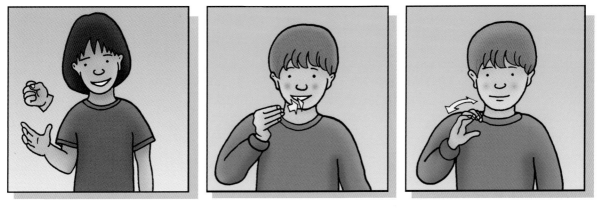

Milk   **Eat/food**   **Drink**

More   **All gone**   **Full**

Cold

ACTIVITIES

Let's eat some more!

- The sign UP can mean, 'Would you like to be picked up?' or 'I want to get out of my high chair!' When your child reaches his hands up to get out of his chair, ask and sign 'UP?' Then pick him up.

- Every time you put your little one in the high chair, car seat or buggy, sign SIT. Eventually you will be able to use this sign when you want him to sit down somewhere.

- Narrate your daily activities for your baby. Sign COOK when you are preparing a meal. Get him involved by giving him some pots and pans of his own to play with while he watches you.

- Say, 'Let's WASH our hands before we eat,' and make the sign for WASH HANDS. Like all the washing and dressing signs, this is a simple miming action.

- Incorporate the food signs APPLE, BANANA, BISCUIT, BREAD, CAKE, CEREAL or ICE CREAM according to what interests your child. Let him be your guide.

- Why not offer your child a choice on occasion? Sign and say, 'Darling, which do you WANT? An APPLE or a BANANA?' He will have no problem showing you.

- Does your baby love to throw things down from his high chair? Ifshe does, this is a great opportunity to introduce DOWN and UP. As he throws his toy down, sign DOWN. Then sign UP and pick it up again.

+ Additional signs

Bread

Cereal

Cake

Up   Sit   Cook

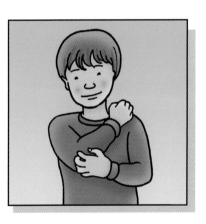

Apple   Banana   Biscuit

Ice cream   Want   Down

ACTIVITIES

My favourite people

- Point to your baby's favourite people and name and sign them. Using signs for important people helps him clearly identify who is who.

- An alternate sign for MUMMY is to tap three fingers on the side of your forehead.

- To identify the different set of grandparents, you can add your own made-up sign names. For example, if maternal Grandma always reads stories to your baby, you can call her GRANDMA STORY to help your baby relate to the differences between her and paternal Grandma.

- You can invent sign names for all the special people in your baby's life. You can do this by inventing a movement or gesture that depicts a behaviour or feature of that person so that your child will recognise and remember it. Do not forget to write these special signs down in your *Invented signs* page at the back of this book. Try not to change the sign or you will confuse your child.

- And why not add the signs YOU and ME to your signing repertoire?

For more on inventing signs, see page 134.

For more on inventing signs, see page 134.

Additional signs

Grandma

Grandpa

Family

Mummy

Daddy

Brother

Sister

Baby

Friend

Me

You

ACTIVITIES

Home, sweet home!

- Within the home, there are many signing opportunities. For example, you can say and sign, 'Shhh! MUMMY is on the TELEPHONE.'

- Use DADDY and WORK to tell your child that Daddy has gone to work, and you can also reassure him that DADDY will return HOME.

- Say, 'Would you like some MUSIC?' Sign WANT and MUSIC.

- As you go through your day, give your baby a running commentary of what you are doing, signing all the key activities.

- Respond to your baby's hiccups, burps, grunts and groans with a surprised expression. Say and sign, 'What was that NOISE?' or 'What a funny NOISE!'

- Show an interest in sounds, like a bell ringing or dog barking, by using the sign for NOISE and the sign for the cause of the noise (TELEPHONE, MUSIC, TELEVISION, etc.).

- If a sound startles your child, sign SCARED after NOISE.

- When you are sitting together, ask your child, 'Do you WANT to read a BOOK or PLAY a game?', using an enquiring expression.

- When the house is untidy, sign and say, 'The HOUSE is DIRTY.' And when you have just completed the housework, sign and say, 'I have FINISHED. The HOUSE is all CLEAN!'

+ Additional signs

Want

Book

Play

Home/house

Work

Telephone

Television

Hear/noise

Music

Scared

Clean

Dirty

ACTIVITIES

Keeping baby safe!

- PAIN/HURT is an abstract concept and does not have a tangible object to support the word. The best way to introduce the PAIN sign is to demonstrate it when you hurt yourself. If you stub your toe, make a pained expression, sign PAIN over your toe and say, 'Ouch!' When your baby bumps himself, sign PAIN over the body part that has been hurt and say, 'Ouch!' Use facial expression to reinforce the sign.

- If you suspect your baby has teething pain, make the PAIN sign by your own cheek, then make it by your baby's cheek. Say 'Ouch' as you make the sign.

- With older babies, you can search for the pain. Point to different parts of the baby's body and ask him if it hurts while you are making the PAIN sign.

- The DON'T TOUCH sign is a very useful sign to warn your child not to touch harmful objects. Most children clearly understand the sign NO (a strong shaking of the head with a look of disapproval). This is why the DON'T TOUCH sign is so effective in preventing potentially harmful outcomes.

- To help your baby to understand HOT, show him the hot tap and make the DON'T TOUCH sign.

- Every time your child is ill, sign and say, 'You are ILL, darling. Let me give you some MEDICINE.'

- If your child has a cough, you can sign and say, 'You have a COUGH, darling. Let's go to the DOCTOR.'

- If you can see your baby struggling with an activity, say and sign, 'Would you like some HELP?' with an enquiring expression.

+ Additional signs

Cough

Doctor

Fire

Hot

Hurt/pain

Touch-no! = Don't Touch

Stop/wait!

Ill

Medicine

Danger

Help

Out and about

- Use the signs for CAR, BUS and WALK, depending on how you are travelling.

- Become familiar with the various modes of transport that you see in your area, and focus on one or two signs each time you go out.

- Your baby will no doubt build up a fine collection of toy vehicles. You can join in the play, introducing the signs for BOAT, AEROPLANE and TRAIN. Show the signs, roar like the engines and have a jolly signing time! Remember to follow your baby's attention. He will be far more motivated to learn if he is directing the focus of interest.

- When you and your baby are looking for your car in the car park, say and sign, 'WHERE is the CAR?' Each car you pass that does not belong to you, say and sign, 'NO, not this one.' When you finally reach it, point and say, 'That's our CAR!'

- Every time you pass or see a bus, point and sign 'BUS'. If you are waiting for a bus and see it coming, say and sign, 'Here COMES the BUS!'

- When you are carrying your child, say and sign, 'Jeremy, I'm putting you DOWN. Why don't you WALK to the corner (or object)?' Point to the corner (object). Then, when you arrive at the corner (object), say and sign, 'Do you want to come UP?'

- When you see a boat in a book, or in real life, show your baby and say/sign BOAT. You can always add BIG or LITTLE BOAT.

- Going to the airport will provide plenty of opportunities to sign and say 'AEROPLANE!' Every time you hear an aeroplane flying overhead, point upwards and say and sign, 'AEROPLANE'.

- Trains and planes often appear in books and provide a great opportunity to introduce those signs. Then, when you see the real thing, your signs will help your baby to connect the picture to the actual object.

+ Additional signs

Come   **Go**   **Down**

Car

Bus

Walk

Boat

Aeroplane

Train

Up

Big

Little

ACTIVITIES

Down the garden path...

- Take the cue from your child. Let him explore, and have the signs at your fingertips for the things that may interest him (FLOWER, BEE, BALL, BIRD, SPIDER etc.).

- Little ones get very excited about SLIDES and SWINGS. Show him these signs just before you go out into the garden, then again when you are playing on the slides and swings. Sign FINISHED just before you have to go inside again so that your child can prepare himself to be torn away!

- Focus on one or two signs each time you go out.

- Play *WHERE is the BALL?* with your baby. This could turn into a lively game of hide and seek while the two of you embark on a botanical adventure, exploring all the backyard delights and using the signs for WHERE, BALL, and all the things you see.

- Say and sign to your child, 'Put on your HAT (or COAT) before you go out and PLAY.' You will find these signs in the Getting Dressed section, page 48.

- What are you going to do when you are outside? Run? Jump? Play? For inspiration, turn to the Action signs, page 66.

+ Additional signs

Bee

Bird

Butterfly

Garden   **Swing**   **Slide**

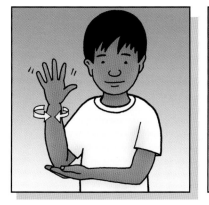  

Tree   **Flower**   **Ball**

Spider   **Worm**

What should we do?

- The following game is useful in helping your child understand that people can disappear and come back again. Firstly, say and sign to your child, 'I am going to GO now, and then I am going to COME back.' Go across the room, and then quickly return to your original position. Repeat this, each time, retreating a bit further, until you finally disappear out of your baby's sight. Reappear with a big smile, a few moments later. Your baby will be reassured that your disappearance is not permanent. These signs will be useful later to explain that a parent is going away but will return.

- Use the LOOK/SEE sign whenever you wish to show your baby something new. If he points to something, sign and say, 'What do you SEE?' Have the signs handy for all the objects that interest your child.

- Whenever you bring out his toy basket, or get him ready for a play activity, sign PLAY. You can add the sign for a favorite toy.

- Each time you are about to go shopping, use the SHOP sign just before you go. While you are selecting items for your basket, sign SHOP just before you choose an item and place it in your basket.

- Use the SWIM, DANCE and JUMP signs when you take your baby swimming, when you listen to music or when he tries to jump. Never forget: children learn best when they observe *you* engaging in the action, so why not rediscover the child in you and have a bit of fun?

- At the end of a busy day, sign and say to your child, 'It's time to SLEEP.' Use SLEEP whenever you see a person or an animal engaged in slumber. This is a handy sign to have - there will come a time when your child approaches you with tired eyes and surprises you with the SLEEP sign!

+ Additional signs

Shop

Swim

Jump

Come

Go

Run

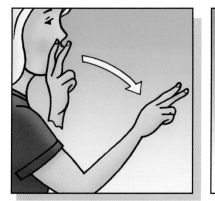

Look/see

Dance

Play

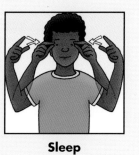

Sleep

It's raining cats and dogs!

- You can look through the window and comment on the conditions outside by saying and signing SUN, RAIN, WARM, HOT or COLD.

- When you are outside, you can say and sign, 'My, it's HOT! Let's stay out of the SUN.'

- When putting on warm clothes, you can sign, 'It's COLD outside. Your HAT and COAT will keep you WARM.'

Additional signs

Hat

Coat

Sun

Rain

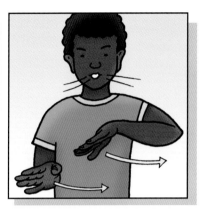

Wind

Snow

Warm

Cold

ACTIVITIES

Fun in the sun!

- Sign and say to your child, 'We are going on HOLIDAY!' to let him know that there are exciting times ahead. Use animated facial expressions.

- Sign GO and SEA and say, 'We are going to the seaside' as you leave your car and are walking towards the beach. Then point to the ocean and say and sign, 'Look, it's the SEA!'

- Allow your baby to run his fingers through the sand. Say and sign 'SAND'. If sand gets on a clean blanket, you can say and sign, 'The SAND is DIRTY'. As you shake the sand away, say and sign, 'CLEAN'. Using one sign in many different events will clearly show your child the many uses of a sign and help to reinforce them.

- If you build a sandcastle, point to it and sign/say, 'SANDCASTLE'. When you have finished building the castle, say and sign, 'FINISHED!'

- It will not take too long for your baby to learn the sign for ICE CREAM. Show him the sign for ice cream, give him some, and you may regret ever having done so!

- Just before you bring out the bucket and spade, say and sign, 'BUCKET AND SPADE', then produce the items. As you are putting them away, sign and say, 'FINISHED', then sign BUCKET AND SPADE as you put them away.

- When you see a seagull, point, make the sign for BIRD and say, 'There is a seagull!'

- When you see a boat or a crab, point at each of them, make the sign and say, 'Look at the BOAT!' or 'Look at the CRAB!'

- Don't forget to use your weather signs at the beach! (See the Weather signs, page 68.)

+ Additional signs

Boat

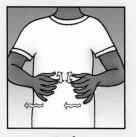
Crab

Seagull (bird)

Holiday

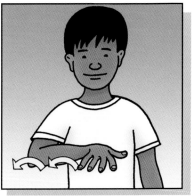

Sea

Sand

Castle/sandcastle

Ice cream

Bucket & spade

Clean

Dirty

ACTIVITIES

Going to the zoo

- Use a book on zoo animals to practise animal signs with your child. The signs will quickly become second nature to you. This process will help you and your child prepare for your zoo experience!

- Every time you see a jungle animal, use it as a signing opportunity.

- Let your baby's interests guide you. Focus on the signs that interest him.

- If the animal moves or makes a sound that makes an impression on him, retell the experience to other family members or friends later that day, making the sign and adding the movement or sound. You can mime or sign actions like scratching, stretching, growling, climbing, swimming, sleeping, and walking.

- If you come across an animal and cannot find a sign for it, look for the animal's most significant characteristic and mimic that feature, using your hands.

- You can add the signs BIG and SMALL when you point out large and small animals to your child.

+ Additional signs

Giraffe

Crocodile

Big

Tiger

Snake

Monkey

Hippo

Lion

Elephant

Small

Mum, I'm feeling...

- When your child cries, or is upset, you can let him know you are aware of his feelings by saying and signing, 'Jeremy is SAD'. Sign HUG to let him know you want him to feel better.

- Say and sign 'HAPPY' during happy times, and allow your face to show the delight you feel.

- As your baby becomes more aware of different feelings, you can add the signs ANGRY, CRY and SCARED.

- When he is angry, ask, 'Are you ANGRY?'

- When something startles him, pretend to be startled too, and sign 'SCARED'. Ask, 'Did that SCARE you?'

- If you see another child crying, point to the child and sign CRY. Say, 'Look! The baby over there is crying.'

- When you are tired, show an exhausted expression and say and sign TIRED just as you are about to sit for a short rest.

- Don't count on your child telling you that he is tired too often. Except, perhaps, during walks so that he can be picked up and carried! Sign and say to him, 'Are your legs TIRED? Okay, I will pick you UP.'

- Starting and ending each day with 'I LOVE you' will quickly help your child learn these signs. When the sign is returned to you, all your effort will be richly and instantly rewarded.

+ Additional signs

Hug   Tired

Happy

Sad

Scared

Angry

Love

Cry

ACTIVITIES

Rub-a-dub dub...

- When it is time for your child to have a bath, using the sign for BATH will help him prepare for the event.

- The *wash* signs such as WASH FACE, WASH HAIR and WASH FEET are simply miming actions.

- To help your baby understand the difference between HOT and COLD WATER, play a game with plastic cups containing warm and cold water. Get his fingers wet, use the signs and say the words. He will quickly learn to let you know if the bath is too hot or too cold.

- Children love using the SOAP sign, so model it as often as is possible.

- As you are bathing your child, make signing a game. Sign and say, 'DIRTY FEET' (make a 'dirty feet' face), 'WASH FEET' (scrub his feet), 'CLEAN FEET' (show him a big smile).

- Learn or create signs for all the bath toys (such as BOAT). For signs like CROCODILE and DUCK, see Jungle and Farmyard Animals pages 74 and 72.

- When the bath is finished, you can sign FINISHED.

- Say and sign 'TOWEL' as you take it off the rail. Then, when you have dried him, sign and say, 'You are DRY now'.

- Don't forget to use the TOILET sign whenever you see your child relieving himself. You will find it useful for later toilet training.

+ Additional signs

Wet

Dirty

Boat

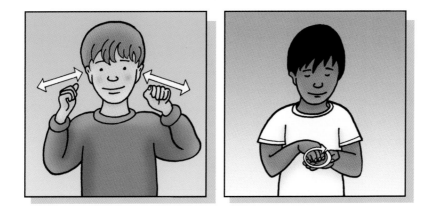

Towel

Soap

Bath

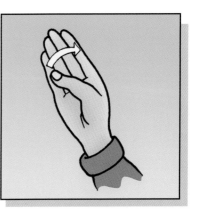

Clean

Water

Dry

Hot

Cold

Toilet

ACTIVITIES

Night, night!

- You have come to the end of a long day. Let your child know that you are TIRED. Explain that it is time for him to SLEEP too and that he should get into BED. Bed and sleep may not seem attractive prospects to your child, but one day he will surprise you by signing SLEEP or TIRED!

- Play bedtime with his toys to reinforce bedtime signs. For instance, sign and say to him, 'Your TEDDY BEAR is TIRED! He wants to go to SLEEP.'

- Show him that it is DARK and there is a MOON outside.

- Let him help you turn off the LIGHT. Children will often learn and use the sign for LIGHT when they want their light kept on during the night. You can combine NIGHT and LIGHT to mean a dim nightlight.

- Add signs like HUG and BLANKET after he is in bed. You can always sign and say, 'WHERE is your BLANKET?' if he has a special blanket.

- Sign BOOK just before reading books and BOOK FINISHED when you are done. If you improvise stories, use the STORY sign instead of BOOK.

+ Additional signs

Blanket

Dark/night

Light

Bed

Tired

Story (book)

Hug/cuddle

Teddy bear

Sleep

Love

Moon

ACTIVITIES

Games – a winning formula

Playing games with your baby throughout the day is not only a great way to interact with your child, it is also a wonderful way to use signs and to introduce new vocabulary and concepts.

To make your baby signing experience a real delight, here are some games to build into your daily routines. If you are playing games with your child already, it will just be a matter of adding signs.

Games can be played anywhere, any time. You can use them when you need a distraction, or when you have a few minutes between events.

Young children love the repetitive and predictable nature of games. They love knowing what comes next, so playing them more regularly will make them more familiar and more enjoyable to your child.

The guidelines given below for the following games are no more than guidelines, so please do not limit yourself. You may find variations of your own that work better for you. Just allow your imagination and creativity to take over - and above all, have fun!

Game 1 – Where's Mummy?

Objective: The purpose of this game is to help your baby learn to identify the names of important people in her life using signs.

How to play:

1. Begin by identifying who is present for the game. 'Look Elisabeth - there's MUMMY (or DADDY)!'

2. Now Mummy or Daddy hides behind the doorway. 'Elisabeth, WHERE is MUMMY? (sign WHERE and MUMMY).

3. If your baby is between 4 and 11 months old, pause for just a moment and then answer the question for her.

4. Mummy or Daddy now jumps out with a smile, and you say, 'There's MUMMY (or DADDY)!' while making the sign for the appropriate person.

Note:

If your child is older or is pointing, pause longer in between to allow her a moment to process the question, point or direct you toward the person hiding. A simple, silent count to three in your head is sufficient. Younger babies do not understand, until they are much older, that when an object/person leaves the room, they still exist, only in a different location. Keep the game light, playful and fast-paced so as not to frighten your child.

Where

Mummy

Daddy

Sister

Brother

Grandma

Game 2 – Where's Teddy?

Objective: The purpose of this game is to assist your baby in identifying objects or animals using signs. It teaches infants to understand that an object has not disappeared permanently just because it is not visible at that moment. She will eventually learn that permanence also applies to people.

How to play:

1. Begin by setting out some of your baby's favourite toys - for example, a favourite stuffed teddy, a toy boat.

2. If your baby is between 4 and 8 months, ask and answer the questions with only a small pause in between. Sign and ask, 'WHERE is TEDDY?' Pause, then answer and point to Teddy, signing, 'There's TEDDY!' After a few times, your child may begin to move towards the hidden teddy. Allow her to find the bear as she catches on to the game.

3. Repeat for each object/toy as you go around the circle of objects.

Note:

Your can replace the given signs with other ones of your choice. If your child is older or is pointing, pause longer in between to allow her a moment to process the question, and then point or answer the question. A simple, silent count to three in your head is sufficient time.

Where

Teddy bear

Boat

Duck

Dog

Cat

Variation – Hide and seek with toys

Objective: This game reinforces object signs.

How to play:

1. Begin by setting out some of your baby's favourite toys or objects - for example, a favourite teddy, a toy truck.

2. Take a blanket or cloth/towel and cover one object at a time.

3. Each time you cover an object ask, 'WHERE is TEDDY?'. Depending on your baby's age, allow her to pull the cloth or covering off for herself. Then answer, 'Yes - there's TEDDY!' For younger babies, simply ask the question, pausing momentarily. Then pull the covering off the object, and answer the question for them.

4. Celebrate with your baby's giggles!

Where

Teddy bear

Boat

Duck

Dog

Cat

Game 3 – Do we eat our socks?

Objective: This game is a fun and light-hearted way to show your baby the approriate things to put in her mouth.

How to play:

Planned play:

1. Set up several items or simply use what you are wearing or sitting near.

2. Sign and ask, 'Do we EAT our SOCKS?' Pretend to eat the socks – sign EAT and pretend to chew. Then answer the question, signing and saying, 'NO, we don't EAT our SOCKS.' For signing YES or NO, nod or shake your head.

Spontaneous play:

1. Let's say baby is about to put a toy in her mouth. You can say, 'Tina! Do we EAT your HAT?' while signing EAT and HAT.

2. Pause, or as you are removing the object, sign, 'NO, we don't EAT your HAT.'

Note:

Feel free to replace these signs with others of your choice. This game can bring hours of fun. Do not think that anything is too obvious to your child. The younger she is, the more helpful this game can be when you need to get her attention quickly and when you are teaching her what does, and does not, go in her mouth. The older your baby is, the more playful and amusing it is for her. Be sure to pause for your older baby to answer the question and to acknowledge her efforts to sign in response.

Socks	**Shoes**	**Hat**

Apple	**Banana**	**Biscuit**

Game 4 – Little person says jump!

Objective: This game is to assist your baby in understanding the connection between signs and action.

How to play:

1. When your baby is younger, this will require more than one person. Person 1 holds the baby facing Person 2. It may be useful to use a baby carrier. Person 2 then uses the sign for SIT. Person 1, holding the baby, sits. When your baby is older, take turns allowing her to be the one to tell you what to do.

2. Now, Person 1 (holding the baby) gives directions and signs at the same time. For example: 'Baby says JUMP!'

3. Upon hearing the direction Person 2 begins to jump.

4. Person 1 says and signs, 'Mummy says SIT'.

5. Person 2 stops jumping and sits.

6. Repeat for different actions.

Note:

Feel free to replace these signs with others of your choice. You may also introduce the sign MORE and ask your baby, in between directions, if she would like to do it once MORE? Another useful sign to use is STOP. On hearing this word and seeing the sign, your baby will feel the sensation in her body and begin to understand the meaning of STOP.

| Dance | Jump | Walk |

| Sit | Sleep | Stand |

GAMES

Game 5 – Let's go to the shops!

Objective: This game is designed not only to help with identifying food signs but also to facilitate a calmer mealtime, when your baby is hungry and not in a terribly tolerant mood.

How to play:

1. Begin by asking your baby, 'Are you hungry? Do you want to EAT?' Make the sign for EAT. Then, with your baby in your arms or seated in a place where she can see everything, pretend that you are going shopping in your kitchen.

2. Sign and say, 'Let's GO to MUMMY'S SHOP! What shall we EAT?' Now begin to sign and select the foods you will prepare for this snack or mealtime.

Note:

Feel free to replace the food signs with others of your choice. Ideally, by making the preparation of food a game, your baby will be more interested in watching you than she will be impatient. Including her in the 'conversation', even if it is one-sided, is a wonderful way to introduce or reinforce new signs.

Eat

Milk

Bread

Cereal

Go

Shop

Game 6 – What does Teddy want to eat?

Objective: This game introduces and/or reinforces food signs and mealtime signs to your baby.

How to play:

1. Choose one of your baby's favorite toys. A doll or stuffed animal is preferable.

2. Pretend to feed the toy as you would your baby. 'Teddy, would you like to EAT?' and 'Would you like MORE MILK?'

3. Take a few turns yourself and then allow your baby to have a turn.

Note:

You can replace the food signs with others of your choice. Once your baby has played this game with you, she will be happy to play it on her own. This game can be a good way to alleviate impatience while you prepare her meal.

Eat	Drink	More

Apple	Banana	Finished

89

Game 7 – Talking on the telephone

Objective: This is a playful activity that reinforces relationship and activity signs.

How to play:

1. Begin by pretending to have a telephone, or using a toy telephone.

2. Have phone ring, answer it and then sign to your baby, 'It's GRANDPA (or GRANDMA) on the TELEPHONE!'

3. Have a pretend conversation with 'Grandpa' (or 'Grandma'), discussing with 'him' (or 'her') what your next activity for the day will be. For example, you might say, 'Yes, GRANDPA, we are going into the GARDEN!' or 'We are about to have a BATH.' Or you may simply hand your baby the phone and say, 'It's your turn. Would you like to say "Hi" to GRANDPA?' At this point, you interpret for you baby. 'Tell GRANDPA I am having a BATH.'

Note:

Feel free to replace these signs with others of your choice. Take your cue from your baby. Sometimes, she will be happy to hear what you have to say, so in that event you can model the signs in the pretend conversation. At other times she will want to do the talking, so you can narrate with signs as she holds and 'talks' on the phone.

Grandpa

Grandma

Telephone

Play

Garden

Bath

Game 8 – I see...!

Objective: This game reinforces the signs for various objects.

How to play:

1. As you go about your day, in the house or outside, you can play this game. Identify an object and guide your baby toward that object. Begin by saying and signing 'Emma, I SEE a BIRD! Do you SEE the BIRD? WHERE is the BIRD?'

2. If your baby is young, pause only momentarily and then show her the bird. If your baby is older, pause longer and allow her to find it himself.

3. When you locate the object for your younger baby, or your older baby has located the object, sign it again: 'Yes - there's the BIRD!'

Note:

Feel free to use other signs of your choice.

See	Where	Aeroplane

Bird	Butterfly	Spider

Game 9 – Puppet on a plate

Objective: This game is to introduce and reinforce feelings and emotions.

How to play:

1. Using a thick black marker, draw a simple, smiling face with bold features on one side of an uncoated, white paper plate. Draw a sad face on the other side.

2. Hold the happy face eight to ten inches (20 to 25 centimetres) from your baby's eyes. When she has focused on it, slowly move it from side to side, and up and down, to see if she is tracking the face with her eyes.

3. Show her the sad side and watch her reaction. Say and sign, 'Lisa is SAD.' Then do the same with HAPPY, SCARED and ANGRY. Use lots of facial expressions.

4. If you like, punch a hole in the top of the plate, thread a string through the hole, and hang the toy where it can turn freely and your baby can see it from her bouncy seat.

Sad

Happy

Scared

Cry   **Love**   **Angry**

Let's rhyme, let's sign!

Your baby will not be able to resist a good rhyme. When he is younger, he will love the sound of the rhythm and repetition of rhyme. As he gets older, the silliness of the words and stories will be very appealing.

Rhymes are not as silly as they seem, though. They are the perfect way to introduce signs to your baby in a fun and relaxed way. They also play an important role in your baby's language development and will greatly assist him in vocabulary and reading later in life.

Below are a few well-known nursery rhymes and some other little ditties to start with. If you are signing to rhymes or songs, you do not have to sign each word in the song. That would be difficult, even for the most seasoned signer! Just select the key words in the sentence. One key word per sentence is usually enough.

How to sign a rhyme

- Before you start, familiarise yourself with each of the signs.

- Go through them with your child a few times so that he can get accustomed to the movements.

- If necessary, support him with forming the signs.

- Sing the rhyme and, as you do, model the signs. Have no fear about embarrassing yourself. The more amusing and ridiculous you are, the more entertainment you will provide for your child.

- Don't be concerned if your child does not make the sign correctly, or does not sign at all. He is taking it all in and becoming familiar with the procedure.

- Praise your child for his efforts.

Be warned! Your child may find rhyming and signing such a fun and entertaining experience that he may want to do it all the time. But, why not be a sport and oblige him? After all, repetition is the key to success!

If you're happy and you know it

If you're happy and you know it, clap your hands.   **HAPPY** *(clap hands)*

If you're happy and you know it, clap your hands.   **HAPPY** *(clap hands)*

If you're happy and you know it,   **HAPPY**

And you really want to show it,

If you're happy and you know it, clap your hands.   **HAPPY,** *(clap hands)*

Happy

Oh where, oh where?

Oh where, oh where is Rory's shoe?   **WHERE, SHOE**

What shall we do, what shall we do?

Oh where, oh where is Rory's Ted?   **WHERE, TEDDY**

Maybe he's here, under the bed   **LOOK, BED**

Oh where, oh where is Rory's book?   **WHERE, BOOK,**

Let's have a look, let's have a look.   **LOOK**

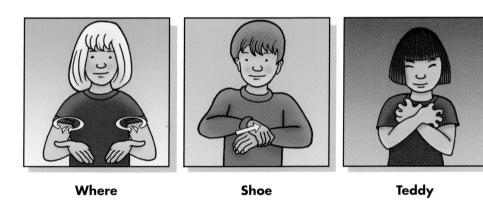

Where   **Shoe**   **Teddy**

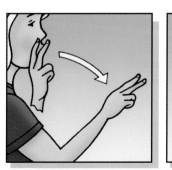

Look   **Bed**   **Book**

Incy Wincy Spider

Incy Wincy Spider climbed the waterspout.   **SPIDER** *(show climbing)*

Down came the rain and washed the spider out.   **RAIN**

Out came the sun and dried up all the rain.   **SUN**

Incy Wincy Spider climbed up the spout again.   **SPIDER** *(show climbing)*

Spider   **Rain**   **Sun**

Wriggle, wriggle little worm

Wriggle, wriggle, little worm,	**WORM**
On a leaf you like to squirm.	**WORM**
Flutter, flutter, butterfly,	**BUTTERFLY**
How is it you fly so high?	**BUTTERFLY**
Slither, slither, curly snake,	**SNAKE**
Do you hiss when you're awake?	**SNAKE**
Gentle cow, that says moo, moo,	**COW**
May we have some milk from you?	**MILK**
Sing, sing, little bird,	**BIRD**
That's the best song I have heard.	

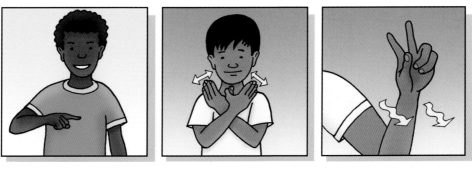

Worm   **Butterfly**   **Snake**

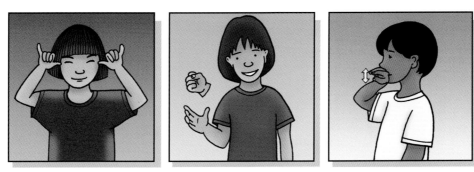

Cow   **Milk**   **Bird**

Caterpillar, caterpillar

Caterpillar, caterpillar, how you squirm and squirm!   **WORM**

Caterpillar, caterpillar, you look like a worm.   **WORM**

One day you will go to sleep,   **SLEEP**

And time will pass you by.

When you awake, you will have wings,   **WAKE UP**

And be a BUTTERFLY!   **BUTTERFLY**

Worm

Sleep

Wake up

Butterfly

This little piggy went to market

Wiggle each of your baby's toes starting with the big toe.

This little piggy went to market.	**PIG, SHOP**
This little piggy stayed at home.	**PIG, HOME**
This little piggy had roast beef.	**PIG, EAT**
This little piggy had none.	**ALL GONE**
This little piggy ran wee wee wee,	**PIG**
All the way home.	**HOME**

(End up running your fingers up his body
and watch him squeal with delight.)

Pig   **Shop**   **Home**

Eat   **All gone**

My buzzing aeroplane

Fly up high and fly down low, buzzing aeroplane,   **AEROPLANE**

Fly in sunshine, fly in wind and fly in pouring rain.   **SUN, RAIN**

Up and down, up and down,   **UP, DOWN**

This is how you fly.   **AEROPLANE**

Buzzing, buzzing, zooming, zooming,   **AEROPLANE**

High up in the sky!

Aeroplane

Sun

Rain

Up

Down

Row, row, row your boat

Row, row, row your boat,

Gently down the stream.

Merrily, merrily, merrily, merrily,

Life is but a dream!

(This rhyme is most effective if you
sit your baby on your lap.)

BOAT

*(Hold his hands and make a
rowing motion)*

Boat

A nappy-changing rhyme

One, two, three, look at Mummy.

Four, five, six, we're going to get this nappy fixed.

Seven, eight, nine, where's the straight line?

From the tummy to the nose is where the straight line goes

Ten, ten, ten, we'll do this again!

LOOK, MUMMY

NAPPY, CLEAN

(with one finger, draw a line from baby's nose to belly button)

MORE

Note:

Sing and sign this rhyme only while you are changing your baby's nappy. If he knows that the only time he will hear the rhyme is during this activity, it will facilitate the nappy process and hold his interest longer. You may not be able to remove one hand during the process, but do not let this concern you. If you do the rhyme with the signs occasionally, your baby will remember them. As he gets older, he may do the signs for you when your hands are busy. Just use the signs with the rhyme as often as you can.

| **Look** | **Mummy** | **Nappy** |

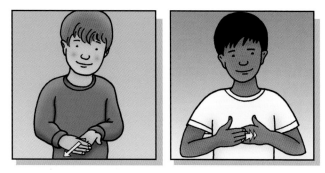

| **Clean** | **More** |

What do we see?

Let's look in the tree and what do we see?	**LOOK, TREE**
A little red bird with her babies three.	**BIRD**
Let's look on the mat - there's a big black cat.	**CAT**
She's cleaning her fur: oh, isn't she fat?	**CAT**
Let's look on the floor, behind the door.	**LOOK**
Old brown dog's asleep with his head on his paw.	**DOG**
Let's look on the log - there's a big green worm.	**WORM**
I wonder if we can see him squirm?	**WORM**

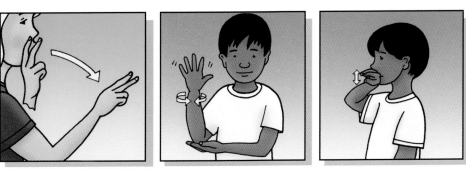

Look	Tree	Bird

Cat	Dog	Worm

The teddy bear family

Mummy Teddy's kind and warm,

Daddy Teddy's strong.

Grandpa Ted and Grandma Ted

are there when things go wrong.

Give hugs to all the children,

and to Mum and Dad.

Let's all have some happy hugs

so we don't get sad.

MUMMY

DADDY

GRANDPA, GRANDMA

HUG

MUMMY, DADDY

HUG

SAD

Mummy

Daddy

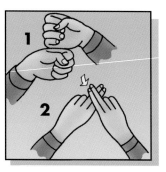

Grandpa

Grandma

Hug

Sad

On the farm

What does the farmer ask the cow?   **COW**

Please may I have some milk from you now?   **MILK**

What does the farmer ask the goat?   **GOAT**

Please may I stroke your furry coat?   **GENTLE**

What does the farmer say to the cat?   **CAT**

Why do you sleep all day on the mat?   **SLEEP**

Cow	Milk	Goat

Gentle	Cat	Sleep

Lucy's feet

Lucy's feet are walking,
Where will Lucy walk?
(Into the garden, etc.)
Lucy's hands are clapping,
Why does Lucy clap?
(Because she's happy)
Lucy's tummy's hungry,
What will Lucy eat?
(Apple, banana etc)

WALK *(Point to baby's feet)*
WALK
GARDEN
(Clap baby's hands together)

HAPPY
(Point to tummy)
EAT
APPLE, BANANA, ETC

Walk

Garden

Happy

Eat

Apple

Banana

Lucy's arms are hugging,   **HUG**

Who will Lucy hug?   **HUG**

(Daddy, Granny, brother etc)   **DADDY, GRANDMA, ETC**

Lucy's eyes are tired,   *(Point to baby's eyes)* **TIRED**

Where will Lucy go?   **GO**

(To sleep)   **SLEEP**

Hug

Daddy

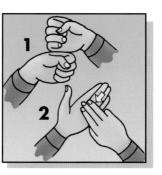

Grandma

Tired

Go

Sleep

Twinkle, twinkle, little star

Twinkle, twinkle, little star,
How I wonder what you are!
Up above the world so high,
Like a diamond in the sky.

Twinkle, twinkle, little star,
How I wonder what you are!

STAR

(Point upwards)
(Make a diamond shape with thumb and forefinger)

STAR

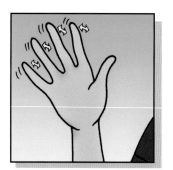

Star

Night night...

'Come to bed,' says Teddy,   **BED, TEDDY**
It's time to say goodnight   *(Blow a kiss to your baby)*
Cuddles for Mum   **HUG, MUMMY**
And hugs for Dad,   **HUG, DADDY**
And please turn out the light.   **LIGHT**

'Keep me safe,' says Teddy,   **TEDDY**
Hold me warm and tight,   **HUG**
Sweetly dream in Dreamland
till the morning light.   **LIGHT**

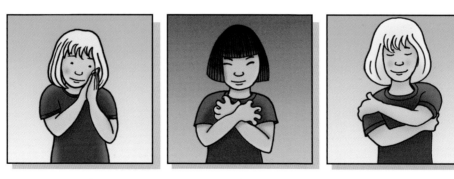

Bed   **Teddy**   **Hug**

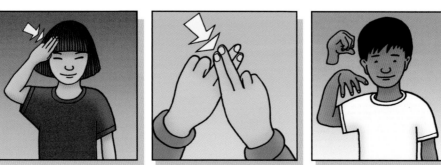

Mummy   **Daddy**   **Light**

Giving books the thumbs up!

Reading books offers endless opportunities to introduce signs. Your child's favourite books will soon become even more endearing to her when you add signing to her reading time. The combination of reading and signing will influence her for a lifetime.

Say and sign 'BOOK' to let her know that it is reading time. Sit her on your lap and make the signs in front of her face between the book and her eyes. Practise some of the signs before you begin reading a particular book, so you are prepared.

Children younger than 18 months tend not to follow a sophisticated story line, but they are attracted to the pictures on the pages. You can begin signing the signs for the characters and objects that appear in the stories.

Make the whole reading experience a joyful one for you and your child. Let her have her blanket or her teddy bear. Give her lots of time to explore the book and take in the signs. Take your cue from her. Let her lead you to the pictures she is most interested in so that you can make the signs for those things. Never try to retain her interest in an object after she has moved on to something new. Eventually, allow your child to make the signs before you make them.

The best types of books are brightly coloured and contain lots of familiar objects and people. Here is a list of some great books to sign with.

Who Says Woof? by John Butler (Puffin)

A beautiful first picture book about farmyard animals.

Signing opportunities include: • CHICKEN • DOG • SHEEP • PIG • COW

Can You Choo Choo Too? by David Wojtowycz (Little Orchard Storybooks)

Again, this is a great first picture book.

Signing opportunities include: • BUS • CAR • PLANE • BOAT

Hello, Lulu by Caroline Uff (Little Orchard Storybooks)

A wonderful first picture book about Lulu, her family and her favourite things.

Signing opportunities include: • MUMMY • DADDY • HOME • DOG • FRIEND • LOVE

Lulu's Busy Day by Caroline Uff (Little Orchard Storybooks)

Meet Lulu again as she plays in the park with the ducks, then returns home for tea, toys and bedtime.

Signing opportunities include: • PARK • SWING • SLIDE • DUCK • HOME • BATH • SLEEP

Lulu's Holiday by Caroline Uff (Little Orchard Storybooks)

Lulu is off to the seaside.

Signing opportunities include:

• HOLIDAY • SWIM • SEA • SANDCASTLE • ICE CREAM

Walking Through the Jungle by Debbie Harter (Barefoot Books)

Be taken on a journey around the world, being chased by different animals.

Signing opportunities include: • LION • SNAKE • BEAR • CROCODILE • MONKEY

I also thoroughly recommend the books written and illustrated by **Annie Kubler** (Child's Play International), which include

Incey Wincey Spider, Baa, Baa, Black Sheep and **Twinkle, Twinkle, Little Star.**

These are excellent signing books for children.

CHAPTER NINE

Your baby's very own book

Creating your baby's own book is a wonderful way to introduce and reinforce signs that are personal and stimulating for your baby.

What to do:

1. On a set of note cards, glue and laminate pictures of family and/or objects that interest your baby. Be sure to include a few written words per page, but no more than three. For example, on a picture of baby with Mummy and Daddy, print the words Mummy, Daddy and [Baby's name].

2. Sign the pictures as you point to each one. Eventually, your baby will enjoy signing her very own book herself.

True Story

When my son Benjamin was 10 months old, I made him a book of signs. This consisted of a laminated page with a word such as CAT in the middle and clip art pictures or photos of cats above the word. Underneath, I put a photo of my older son William, aged four, signing the word CAT, as a way of making William feel involved in the signing process. He couldn't understand why we made a fuss of Benjamin when he put a finger to his cheek if a cat walked past!

This is now Benjamin's favourite book, full of his best-loved things and people. He delights in sitting with his carers at nursery, showing them these signs, and it gives the carers an opportunity to familiarise themselves with, and use, the signs that Benjamin understands. He is now 20 months old and has a signing vocabulary of about 100.

Baby-signing mum Emma, Norfolk

Part III

Frequently asked questions

Using this section

Now that you have started to use signs in your everyday lives, it is inevitable that you will have many questions. For example, you may wonder how many signs to use during a particular event, or what to do if your baby has not started signing after being exposed to signs for several weeks or months, or what happens to the signs once your child begins talking.

In Part III I provide answers to the questions that parents most commonly ask me. These are categorised in five main groups:

- **Moving beyond first signs**
- **Common problems with signing**
- **From signs to speech**
- **For parents of children with special needs**
- **For childcare professionals.**

Following the last section is a collection of enchanting real-life stories that recount some of the experiences of many of Britain's baby-signing parents.

These stories capture the magic of baby signing and serve to illustrate the results that can be achieved with just a little patience and perseverance by using my teaching principles.

Benjamin signs 'brother'

Moving beyond first signs

Q: How many signs should I introduce to my child?

There are no set rules on the number of signs to demonstrate to your child, so this is a personal choice. You may feel comfortable using 100, or it may suit you to use 12. It is worth keeping in mind that you will need to present a lot of signs with consistency and repetition, throughout the day, in order for your child to learn many signs. That way, you are making available to him a broad selection of signs for the ease and benefit of his communication.

Q: Can I overload my child with too many signs?

No. As a parent you would not restrict the number of words you spoke to your child, and the same applies when using signs. You are merely exposing him to language that is presented in two forms – spoken and signed. He will then choose the signs that he most needs and disregard those that he does not need. Using a lot of signs will offer him a wider variety of options, which will later help him to communicate better. The only way that you could overload a child would be to place demands on learning or to make the communication process a lesson rather than simple daily communication.

Q: How many signs will my baby learn before speech takes over?

This depends on many factors, including the child's personality, the environment in which he is raised and the level of exposure to the signs. I have worked with several families whose children were using 100 signs by their first birthday after just a few months of signing. However, others reported that their babies thrived on using between 12 and 25 signs by the first year. Most children seem to acquire and use between 20 and 50 signs before speech takes over.

The general rule is that the more signs your child regularly sees, the more he will use, and the broader the dialogue will be between the two of you. This is not always the case, though. Sometimes a child may be exposed to numerous signs but never make them because he sees no reason to use them. In this instance, he will understand far more signs than he actually uses.

The onset of talking inevitably limits the number of signs your child learns. Those children who use 50 to 100 signs in their first year do not necessarily add many more signs when they start speaking. Most have little use for more signs and tend to drop them altogether when they begin replacing the signs with words.

Q: This sign looks too difficult for my baby to make! Can I use another one?

When showing signs to your baby, the most important question to ask yourself is, 'What sign will best allow communication between him and me?' Obviously, a BSL (British Sign Language) sign is preferable and most BSL signs work well, but some may require using specific finger movements that may be too complex for a very young child to make.

In this case it is best to seek an alternative from another sign language dictionary (such as American Sign Language) or simply make one up. Use the alternative sign with your child to start; then as your child's dexterity develops, slowly add the BSL sign alongside the alternative sign. With time he will realise that both signs carry the same intended meaning, and then you can drop the alternative sign.

Q: Is it possible to use the sign without the word – for example, when I don't want to embarrass my baby in public?

I generally recommend that you reinforce the sign with the word so that your baby can clearly hear and see the connection between the two. However, there are occasions when signs become effective without the spoken words – for example, during peaceful moments, or later in your child's life when you do not wish to embarrass him in public.

In other people's homes, signing SIT DOWN without articulating the words usually brings the required result. In addition, a simple look and a subtle use of the sign STOP could bring a more-or-less immediate halt to inappropriate behaviour, while having the added benefit of preventing you from having to charge across the room.

True Story

I found the STOP sign very effective when I was parenting Ben. When he ran too far ahead of me in the car park, I would call his name, catch his eye, and then sign STOP. It saved me from having to holler like a fishwife and mortify him in public.

Baby-signing mum Helen, Swindon

Signing without words is also helpful when toilet-training your toddler. On the occasions your child is out and about, he will often get so caught up in the excitement of the moment that an accident may occur before he is even aware of what is happening. A sign is a delicate reminder and avoids having to put him on the spot in front of friends.

Signs should not become more than delicate reminders. Parents must take care not to begin using signs as a disciplinary tool. Some folks in the United States did this with their children aged two and under, and rightly caused some consternation. After all, if people are prepared to think of punishing children that young, it is they who are in need of being taught how to behave!

Q: Should I encourage my baby to sign PLEASE and THANK YOU when he asks for something?

I would strongly suggest that you wait until your baby understands the concepts of etiquette and gratitude, around or just after the age of two, before asking him to add the signs PLEASE and THANK YOU. It will only confuse him if he first learns the sign for MILK and uses it successfully, only to be expected later to add the sign PLEASE when he wants some! By the time he begins to understand the purpose of these words, speech is usually taking over, thus avoiding any need to use these signs.

Q: What is the sign for SORRY?

I see many parents attempting to make their babies sign SORRY. Most children only begin to grasp the concept of sorry when they are about three years old, or older – at any rate, beyond the time that they require signs to communicate. I would urge you not to insist that your child sign SORRY before he fully comprehends its meaning. However, you as the parent can use the SORRY sign when you accidentally bump your child or step on a toe. When a parent makes the signs for SORRY, PLEASE and THANK YOU in context, it helps the child develop a foundation for later understanding.

Q: Do babies sign together?

It was always believed that babies did not sign with other babies because social play among children tends to develop when they are around two years old (about the same time that they start to talk). However, I have seen and received countless reports from various baby-signing parents who have made reports to the contrary – namely, that their babies have used, or at least understood, signs made by other babies. This would make sense since children tend to adopt behaviour that they observe in other children. Children may also use some signs with dolls or other toys.

True Story

I was recently at a party with my husband and my son Alex, who is 14 months old and who knows about a dozen signs. The hosts of the party also had a baby who is learning signing and is at a similar stage as Alex. The two boys were playing together on the carpet and our friend's son Adam was eating a cracker. Alex looked at the cracker and signed to Adam EAT and MORE. Adam must have understood, because he crawled over to the bag, leading Alex to the stash of crackers!

Baby-signing mum Sue, Buckinghamshire

Q: Will using signs in a bilingual home confuse the child?

No, not at all. Because signing is visual, it actually assists your baby in seeing the connection between the two differently pronounced words. Research shows that it does not matter how many different languages you bring into your home. Your child may initially mix them up, but with adequate exposure will eventually become fluent in all of them. Multiple language production may require a little more mental processing time.

CHAPTER TEN

Q: Can I combine signs?

Yes, absolutely. Once your child has a few signs at his disposal and is confidently using them, you can begin using two signs together, thereby presenting him with the opportunity to get his message across more effectively. Why not try the following combinations?

- MORE and MILK
- DRINK and ALL GONE
- WHERE? and DOG
- WATER and HOT
- DADDY (MUMMY) and WORK
- DON'T TOUCH and HURT.

Your child will acquire the ability to combine signs from about 14 months old. Children who have an average signing vocabulary of 20 to 50 signs by their first year generally start creating short, signed sentences at around 14 to 17 months – although I have witnessed children as young as one year old producing full short sentences.

True Story

Our son Charlie is 20 months old. He can sign more than 100 words. We have a great story about his progress, using your signing programme. We had just emptied out most of the water in our fish tank because we were moving. The tank was on the floor – all the fish were lying in just a couple of inches of water, and all the plants had fallen over. Charlie looked into the tank and signed this amazing sentence to me: FISH, HELP, TREE, FALL DOWN. It was so cute and funny and allowed me to see more clearly into Charlie's sweet and caring personality. He was so happy that I had understood his concern for the fish.

Baby-signing mum Sam, Notting Hill

Common problems with signing

At some stage of your baby-signing journey you may stumble up against what I call a 'baby-signing block' that will have you scratching your head with frustration. You may very well find, for example, that although you have been signing to your baby for three months she is not signing back, or that she seems to be signing but the signs look nothing like yours.

If you are following my programme and this happens, comfort yourself – you are doing nothing wrong! And neither is your baby. Every child is different and they learn and produce signs at their own pace. Your child is processing language in her brain. That process takes time. Be patient – and keep signing.

Q: Why hasn't my baby started signing yet? We've been showing her signs for a long time now ...

Just because your baby is not signing back, it does not mean that she is not taking it all in. Much of her learning takes place long before she displays any indication that she is learning anything. Her little mind is absorbing, developing and increasing her understanding of the world around her. Every waking moment can produce new perceptions for a baby. As she experiences an event again and again, she develops a visual record, connecting the event to the words and the signs you are making. The more consistent you are when making the signs, the faster she will make the connection. Be patient and never show disappointment. Eventually, she will begin to understand what the signs mean, and when she is ready she will begin to replicate them. The learning process for signing is similar to the learning process for speaking.

Babies develop at different speeds. The onset and amount of language expressed are dependent on factors such as individual personality, the learning environment, and how comprehensively the vocabulary is reinforced by significant people in the child's life. Many factors affect the learning pace for language acquisition. Continuous exposure to the signs and a positive attitude in parenting dynamics greatly contribute to learning. So even though waiting for language to emerge may be frustrating for both you and your child, it is perfectly normal. It is important not to push language on a child. Let the child discover language and its use through her needs, and then she will expand from there. A child may become hesitant if she feels she must perform. At a time when your child is concentrating on learning something else – how to crawl, for instance – she may wait until one skill is solidly attained before beginning a new adventure.

After eight or nine months of parenting most of us are such good parents, and so good at predicting our children's needs, that from the child's perspective there may be very little reason to sign. Parents tend to meet their children's requests all too eagerly, before they have engaged their little minds and take a chance to ask for themselves. Although a parent should never withhold care pending sign production from a child, allowing a few seconds' space and setting up situations that promote sign usage is advantageous to development. Each successful engagement is dramatically important in relation to the next. If you never provide situations that encourage communication, none will result.

You feel you can anticipate her needs, so use your anticipation as a tool. When you notice that your child is thirsty, for instance, instead of handing her a drink, pour it and set it slightly out of reach, in her sight-line. Using the sign, ask her if she would like a drink – and allow a few seconds for a response – never long enough for her to become frustrated, but long enough for her to remember what to do to obtain the drink. Such an approach is invaluable in assisting her to expand her communication skills.

Something else you could try, if an opportunity arises, is to show older children who associate with your child the signs you want your baby to learn. The fastest way to jump-start a baby into communication is to get her to interact with an older sibling or another child with good signing skills. Studies show that given equal time, an older child can teach a younger child sign language much faster than an adult can teach the same child.

Q: My baby makes one sign for everything. What should I do?

Often, a young baby between six and ten months old will make her first sign (perhaps for MILK or MORE) and will discover that the sign gets results. She will then use the same sign for everything. Children frequently go through an identical phase when they are learning to speak, using a word like 'Mama' to cover a whole host of needs. This is perfectly normal and clearly demonstrates your child's understanding that the sign symbolises something. If you are concerned, show her many more signs so that she can see different gestures for different things. She is, at the very least, well on her way to using signs.

Now it is up to you to provide an environment that stimulates communication. Your baby will be surprised when a sign fails to get her the expected results. However, seeing more signs and testing them to see the response she gets will stimulate her understanding that different signs achieve different results.

It is worth remembering that consistency and repetition are the key to helping your baby understand. Keep using the signs in context, and sooner or later she will begin using the correct sign in its correct context.

At the same time it has to be said that some sign hand-shapes do look similar and can be a little confusing to a young baby – like MILK and ORANGE JUICE, for example, which both use a squeezing hand. That is why keeping the signs in context is helpful to your baby and to you while she endeavours to decipher exactly what her first few signs mean. Parents encounter very much the same syndrome again when their child begins speaking – when she tries to say the two words 'ball' and 'bird', for instance, and they both come out as 'bah'!

Q: My baby tries to make all of her signs at once when she wants something!

This is not an uncommon situation when your baby has learned a few signs and is excited about something. Keep making the signs correctly and in context. With time and repetition she will eventually learn to differentiate between the signs. Meanwhile, keep alert to the things that do achieve success and use those to progress further. Communication will improve in time and be well worth your patience.

Q: My baby makes the wrong sign at the wrong time!

If your baby suddenly makes a sign apparently out of context, it may well be that she is thinking about that object. She may be communicating what she would like, or just what has come to mind at that particular moment. Babies often hear a word or see something that sparks interest in something with which they are familiar, and they will comment on or react to it through sign, word or play.

Q: I introduced some signs to my baby, but I have not used them for weeks.

In my own experience with my children, and from what the parents in my classes have told me, your child will still be able to produce the signs despite not seeing or using them for a long time. Children can sometimes make a sign they have seen only once or twice, weeks or even months earlier. However, success with communication is improved with consistent sign use.

True Story

Until Tom was old enough to speak, I had used several signs with him that he had never used himself. For example, he signed PIG, DUCK and HORSE, but never COW or SHEEP. One day when he was in the bath, I showed him the signs for COW and SHEEP without saying the words. He immediately said the words back to me. Then I showed him other signs that he had been shown only once or twice before, many months prior and again he said the correct words. This proved to me that although he had never used these signs, he had absorbed all the information and had understood exactly what each sign meant. I was stunned!

Baby-signing mum Lucinda, Exmouth

Q: My baby doesn't make the sign correctly. What should I do?

You should approach this in the same way you would when demonstrating any language. You should set a standard and hold to it. Your baby's first attempts to sign may look nothing like yours. In fact, hers may look quite clumsy by comparison. This is because before the age of two a baby's dexterity is still developing.

Babies go through a process in which they make a broad attempt to replicate your movements. Then, as they develop dexterity and as they begin to see the differences between their version and your version, they modify their version and more closely mimic your movements. For example, a baby may begin making the signs for MORE by clapping her hands. After a time, she may then learn to close her hands and tap her fingertips together instead of her palms. If you are consistent with your signs, you greatly contribute to her learning and refinement process. Modifying your version of a sign and adopting your child's version may cause problems as her world expands and others who know signs will not recognise hers. (After all, you certainly would not adapt your pronunciation of 'toothbrush' to 'toosfrus' just because your child is temporarily unable to say the word correctly.) In the meantime, while waiting for your child's transformation, show her sign to other family members and caregivers so that they can at least understand her temporary version.

If your child suddenly modifies a sign she already knows well, she may be trying to create a new sign for something or she may see a subtle difference in something and is attempting to reflect that difference with her sign. Be alert for this because it frequently happens.

Q: My childcare provider doesn't use signs. What should I do?

Once childcare providers discover how beneficial baby signing is for reducing noise levels, tantrums and other related problems such as hitting and biting, they may start to implement signing into their programmes. I suggest that you let them know the signs your baby uses so that they are better able to service her needs. Through that experience, they will quickly learn how beneficial signing can be.

Q: I'm the only one in the family using baby signing with my child. My husband and parents are cynical. Will that delay the process?

Signing does not have to include the entire family to work. As long as you are signing on a consistent and regular basis, you are likely to obtain successful results. However, it is obvious that the more involved people who are important to your child become, the faster and richer the communication that results. In one family of my experience, an older child learned some signing at school and brought it home. The child ended up interpreting until the parents finally learned the signs through simply watching.

True Story: To those parents who think it will never take hold ...

We began signing with our daughter Ellie when she was five months old. We used just ten signs, but tried to be consistent, using them every day. Several months went by and when, by her tenth month, she still hadn't attempted to sign, we became resigned and were on the verge of giving up. In despair I sent you an e-mail explaining our predicament – to which you replied: 'You don't stop talking after five months, so why stop signing? Children take time to process language and they will sign when the need causes them to want to draw on their manual language resource.'

Inspired by this, we managed to extend our signing attempts by a further two weeks, yet this motivation then vanished just as rapidly as it had appeared, and we decided to abandon the signing, feeling exhausted and perplexed.

I can only think that Ellie must have sensed our desperation, because the very next day she began making the signs that we'd been showing her all those months. I realise now that she'd simply been absorbing them but hadn't been ready to use them. After that, she was quick to learn and use many more signs, culminating in a maximum of 60 signs before speech took over.

Baby-signing dad Les, Ludlow

From signs to speech

One of the wonderful benefits of using signs as a way to communicate with your baby is that by the time your child is able to speak, he already knows how to use language to navigate through life. Now all he needs to do is begin to play with the new toy at his disposal – his voice.

Q: I've been showing signs to my child, but now he's speaking.
Is it really worth continuing signing?

Yes! When he learns to speak, he will have a multitude of words to learn, some of which are difficult for a beginner to articulate – like 'hippopotamus', for example. Signs bridge the gap and make learning to tell the difference between similar-sounding words – like 'ball' and 'bell' and 'bow' – much easier. Parents often defer using the signs that are replaced by words and after some time start using signs again for fun in games or to communicate through windows or across distances. Signs really come in handy during toilet training, while learning to read and to spell, and as a special family language.

Q: Does the conversion from signs to speech happen overnight?

No. Your child will not go to bed signing and wake up talking! It is a gradual process. At around 12 months his need to speak will become more compelling and he will attempt to say more and more words. But the onset of speech occurs very slowly, and the number of signs he can make dramatically outweighs the number of words he can articulate during this stage. In this way, signs serve as an effective back-up until he is able to articulate the words correctly. As soon as he becomes competent in saying a word, he is likely then to drop the sign.

True Story

Abbie made the sign for ELEPHANT from the age of ten months. At 19 months she began to say what sounded like 'ele-', but it was easy to understand what she meant, because she always made the sign. We would confirm that we understood the word by saying, 'Yes, Abbie – it's an elephant.' It took a great deal of practice before she was able to pronounce the word 'elephant' correctly. In the next few weeks Abbie became more interested in showing off her new word. Although she generally combined the word and the sign, there were several occasions on which she left out the sign altogether. The more confident she became with using the word, the less she would use the sign, until one day she no longer signed. I guess she no longer had any use for it.

Baby-signing mum Sally, Norfolk

CHAPTER TWELVE

Q: What happens to the signs when my baby starts talking?

Normally, your baby will use both signs and speech for a time. Once he masters words, his signing will be reduced. However, there are often situations when signs are still very useful. These include:

- in public, when you wish to avoid embarrassing your child. For example, you could use the TOILET sign when you are toilet training, and the STOP, DON'T TOUCH and GENTLE signs when you need to offer him behavioural guidance.

- as a back-up when he is still having trouble pronouncing a word. The signs can help take the guesswork out of your attempts to understand your child's early speech.

- in a noisy place where it is easier to use the sign than to struggle to hear each other speak

- in a 'no talking' area such as a cinema, church, seminar or library. You can now 'speak' without breaking the silence!

- as a game. Make a sign and then wait for your child to say the correct word or do the correct action.

- to communicate with other people who use sign language. Your child will certainly appreciate knowing a second language without the difficulties older people encounter when learning languages.

- to communicate with new additions to your family who are commencing their own baby-signing journey.

As your child grows older he may or may not choose to hang on to sign language. Whether he does or not, one thing is certain: he will never lose the bond that was created between the two of you through interacting so closely during the first years of his life. On a subconscious level he will never forget the gift that you gave him that allowed him to share his thoughts and needs with you. He will never forget the eye contact, the way you praised him, and the gentle way you helped him form his first few signs. He will never forget the love, the kindness, the understanding. A deep and indestructible bond has been established. And it will continue to get stronger ...

Special children, special adults

FAQs for parents of children with special needs

Q: Was this programme developed for children who are deaf or hard of hearing?

No, it was developed for hearing babies and their parents. However, because it is based on BSL (British Sign Language) it is also beneficial for children who have special needs, including children who are hearing-impaired. If BSL is your child's primary form of communication, she will need other professional support.

Q: Was this programme developed for children with special needs?

Yes. For years, speech-language pathologists have recommended signing for children who have learning disabilities or developmental delays. It has also proved to be successful with children with autism and Down's syndrome. In fact, any child who is unable to speak can benefit from signing. This includes children who have undergone a tracheotomy.

 True Story

My son Sean is 30 months old and has Down's syndrome. Learning signs has reduced his frustration immensely. I wanted Sean to be able to have a structured language system that he could use in the world, not just at home. When people don't understand what he is trying to say, he will often use sign language to clarify his message. We encourage him to talk and sign at the same time. He now knows and uses almost 200 signs.

Baby-signing dad Matt, Catford

Expert opinion

Tania Allen, paediatric speech and language therapist in Kent, says:

Speech and language therapists frequently expose signs to children who have a delay in their language development. This allows them to participate in interaction without relying on their limited spoken abilities. As a consequence, the child is exposed to more conversation, which leads to a significant improvement in his confidence and communication skills. In addition, signing alleviates the sense of frustration and isolation that having a communication difficulty can bring. The use of signing has also been seen to facilitate the development of a child's receptive and expressive language abilities. Parents who use signs with their children alongside spoken language naturally employ the positive interaction strategies of speaking slowly, using key words, being face-to-face, etc. This in turn helps the child to learn new spoken words.

If you would like to read further about the benefits of signing with children with special needs, you can read the relevant references in the background reading section, listed at the end of the book, all of which can be found at major libraries or online.

Q: I am deaf. My child is not. Can I still use your system?

Yes. Signs can be useful to teach hearing children when the parent or parents are hearing, deaf, or hearing-impaired. All children respond to language when provided with an appropriate learning environment. Hearing children of deaf adults (called CODAs in the USA) end up bilingual and become fluent in both signing and speech.

FAQs for childcare professionals

Q: I am a childcare professional. How can baby signing help me?

Many childcare providers who use sign in their classrooms report that signing dramatically improves the environment for children and staff. The most obvious benefit is a quieter classroom, particularly in pre-school settings where signs can replace the distressing noise of whining, crying and tantrums. Removing the guesswork involved in determining the various reasons for these outbursts allows for more time to play, learn, and interact in positive ways.

Choosing a programme that uses both signs and speech will help your child's overall language development. Signs can enhance children's social skills. For example, STOP, SHARE, and GENTLE can be used among children playing together to avoid the disruptions or hurt feelings that often arise. Signs such as ANGRY or SCARED allow children to express their emotional feelings to staff in times of crisis.

Top tips for childcare professionals

- Signing should be a normal part of communication and not presented as a taught subject. Integrate the signs naturally, as part of the children's everyday life in the classroom. Children learn best when they are playing and having fun.

- There is no need to introduce the whole language – just a few key signs during regular events, such as those listed in the Activities section.

- Use the key signs during all activities.

- Small groups are important because they encourage conversation and allow all children to express themselves.

- Always speak the word as you sign so that children learn both the sign and the word.

- Always praise and acknowledge a child's attempts to sign.

- Respond to a child's signing attempts, even if the child's hand-shapes are incorrect, by confirming what he has signed. Do this by forming the sign correctly and pairing it with the word.

- As other children learn and use signs, all children should be encouraged to use their signs with each other, especially for conflict resolution and apologies.

- Encourage children to sign when they are crying. This helps to reduce the length of tantrums and resolve the issue faster.

- Written or printed language should be incorporated into activities to develop literacy. Signs with the accompanying word will help children associate the word/sign/picture relationship.

True stories

One fantastic thing about using sign language with your baby is that you become more articulate when you are communicating with her. In combining the word with the sign, I became more conscious of how I was speaking to Clare. When I said 'nappy', I would repeat 'nappy, nappy, nappy,' over and over again, as slowly and as precisely as I could, using lots of eye contact, making sure that she was observing the sign. I would also exaggerate my facial expressions. Clare speaks very well now. I think showing her how to sign definitely helped!

Baby-signing dad Thomas, Gloucester

We don't have any horror stories of pacing the floor at 3 a.m. with a red-cheeked screaming infant. From an early age, Meadow learned the signs for MEDICINE and TEETH, and soon learned that if she signed both, the teething gel was quickly applied to her gums. At the first sign of pain she would sign for her medicine. We would apply it, and then never had to contend with the screams that are usually the first indicator that a child is teething. As she learned more signs, her frustration levels dropped dramatically.

Baby-signing mum Gill, Inverness

Tina kept a parenting journal as she raised her two children, Tim and Max. Her youngest, Max, received the benefit of sign language whereas her eldest, Tim, did not.

I was astounded at the difference between Tim and Max during their second year of life, mainly in the area of tantrums and confrontations. I recorded a range of twelve to fifteen confrontations a day with Tim, and only six to eight with Max.

There was also a difference with the duration of each confrontation.

Each confrontation lasted half as long when I used sign language with Max. Using signs to specify objects and feelings seemed to resolve situations more quickly. This extra time was put to good use in other activities and helped me to be far more engaging with Max.

Baby-signing mum Tina, Truro

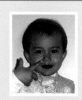

When we were in South Africa in April this year, my mother in law looked after my kids for a week. My daughter Kiara is 5 yrs old and Kagan was approx 15 months at the time. It was the first time that Kagan was away from me for more than a day. Kagan was brilliant, signing with his granny every time his nappy needed a change. Kiara was able to interpret the rest of the signs to her granny, which made caring for him easy.

Baby-signing mum Pamela, Sandhurst

I'd been signing with my son, Sam, for four months and by 11 months of age he still hadn't used a sign himself. I was beginning to feel despondent, so I went to see my baby-signing group leader to see if she could help. As soon as I arrived, I dived into my handbag to give Sam his drink. My teacher stopped me and suggested that I leave the drink in his sight-line, but slightly out of reach. Within a minute Sam made his first sign for DRINK. All it had taken was a few seconds to motivate him into action. The pair of us were in tears, dancing round the room and hugging Sam. I got on the phone straight away to tell Daddy and grandparents. Later that day I was tickling Sam and lo and behold, every time I stopped, he signed MORE. From that day on there was no stopping him! Signs began to pour out of him. He had been absorbing all the signs I was using but just didn't begin expressing himself until he felt he was ready. Once the floodgate was opened, he was on his way.

Baby-signing mum Sara, Swindon

Maria feels that signing has given her an incredibly special bond with her baby Tamara, now 18 months.

Tamara now has a vocabulary of 40 signs and she is starting to form three-word sentences. Through signing she's also been able to display her sense of humour from the tender age of 12 months. For example, she looks through a book and signs all the correct signs for the animals. Then, all of a sudden, she chooses a well-known picture like a cat and deliberately signs DOG, then laughs and shakes her head. It's as though she wants to make sure I am paying attention!

Baby-signing mum Maria, West Wickham

At the age of 13 months Isabella was using 35 signs to communicate with us. She could initiate conversations, sing whole nursery rhymes with her hands, and even crack jokes! One instance to illustrate how bright she was happened when we were out shopping one day. We were standing at the delicatessen of a big store when Isabella started signing RABBIT while staring at the assistant behind the counter. I looked at her, confused, but she continued to sign RABBIT more and more vehemently. I glanced back at the assistant and noticed his mouth. Out of it protruded two of the most enormous bunny teeth you have ever seen! It was a very funny moment. I was amazed at her being able to make such an insightful comparison at such a young age.

Emma of Babysigners, Hove

CHAPTER FOURTEEN

When our baby was eight months old, she used to clap her hands together a lot. my husband and I thought that she was just very happy! Then one day a friend of ours who we had met at a baby-signing workshop noticed Klaudia's clapping and told us that Klaudia was actually making the sign for MORE! She explained that her son Daniel had been unable to form the MORE hand-shape and so had clapped, until his dexterity had matured to the point of correctly forming the sign. Realising that Klaudia had been attempting to sign all of this time, we began noticing that she was also making other signs that we had dismissed as random gestures. However, by observing the context in which she was using the signs, we were able to identify several of the signs that she had so bravely been attempting!

Baby-signing mum Anna, Glastonbury

After weeks of trying the more basic signs of MILK and EAT, which Flora was showing no sign of copying, she decided that her first sign would be FINISHED. I almost danced the first time I saw it. I couldn't believe it! I sent e-mails to the entire family. Amazingly, she did the sign perfectly from the start – so my many repetitions of it, after each meal, had obviously paid off. She looked as pleased as pie when she did it. As pleased as she'd looked when she walked for the first time. Before long she'd acquired a vocabulary of more than 50 signs.

Baby-signing mum Lucy, Oxford

I remember an incident when Joshua was being bullied at school. Although it was dealt with immediately by the teacher, Joshua was understandably reluctant to go to school the next day. Leaving him in the classroom was heart-breaking. The look on his face was so sad, and it took all my willpower not to go in and take him home with me. His eyes were still searching for mine as I left the classroom. As I walked past the window, I simply signed I LOVE YOU to him. None of his friends knew what I'd said, so it didn't embarrass him, and the corners of his mouth twitched into a brave smile.

Baby-signing mum Wendy, Tunbridge Wells

When Ziggy was two, I started using the TOILET sign with him and knew that when he needed to go, he would let me know. Occasionally, I would use the sign for TOILET and he would sign NO. About two months later, he came up to me and signed TOILET and that was it! From that day on, he just let me know whenever he needed to go, and rarely had an accident. He was just 26 months old!

Baby-signing dad Sean, Hampshire

When Mattie is watching television and an animal appears, I make a sign for that animal. Each time a new animal comes on, she turns to me, to give her the sign. It's our little game. She's learned many signs this way. We sometimes make up a sign that mimics the animal's shape or movement. Then when we come across the same animal in a book, we both make the sign and laugh.

Baby-signing mum Sally, Kent

My daughter Imogen was looking out of the window, watching the birds on the feeder, when a squirrel ran up the feeder. She became very excited, and attempted to tell us what was happening. She started signing BIRD, but seemed to know that that wasn't the right sign for the squirrel, so she stopped to think for a moment. A few seconds later she exuberantly signed BIRD and growled at the same time. It was so cute, and more importantly, she got the message across to her mum and me by modifying and adapting what she already knew to a totally new situation. Signing has shown us the extent to which a child thinks and analyses her world before she can speak. What's more, it shows us how creative and imaginative she is!

Baby-signing dad Stephen, Cheltenham

We didn't have a sign for spaghetti, so Poppy decided to use the sign for WORMS instead, to tell us what she wanted for lunch!

Baby-signing mum Sylvia, Devon

I'm invited to lecture on baby signing at medical schools and residency programmes for new doctors. I regularly lecture at hospitals, and many doctors and nurses attend. I have many stories about doctors being suspicious at first, only to become strong advocates of the programme. One vocal doctor who at first was sceptical signed with his own child, and once he'd experienced the benefits, began giving a learning kit to every new parent he met. After 15 years, I have countless stories from paediatricians and developmental psychologists who've begun cautiously and ended up being our best promoters.

Baby-signing dad and author of this book, Joseph, Bellingham (Washington State)

Final words

Countless parents have told me how signing has changed their relationships with their children. Not only does signing with your children reduce frustration for everyone but the depth and quality of such early communication is an experience every family should enjoy. The window of opportunity is short – but the results that can be achieved are extraordinary.

I personally feel that sign language is a wonderful gift from the hearing-impaired community, and that it should be respected as such. At a time when so many people (especially politicians) are doing things that muddle truth and communication, I am proud to offer this map that will enable parents and caregivers to find their way to kindness, understanding and the joy that can come from pure, honest communication with their children. I hope you embrace my work and share my enthusiasm and passion.

I wish you well on your baby-signing journey.

Joseph

Part IV

Show me a sign!

The A to Z of baby sign language

Using this section

This section has 172 of the most commonly used first signs in British Sign Language (BSL). They are in alphabetical order for easy finding, are clearly illustrated with drawings, and are accompanied by simple instructions on how to make each sign.

If you are unable to find a sign in this book, check a BSL dictionary, look online at www.britishsignlanguage.com, or as a last resort invent your own.

When you invent your own sign, though, please remember to make it as simple as possible. If it represents an action, just use a miming gesture. For example, the sign for typing on a keyboard would be a typing action. If the sign represents an object, show the shape of the object with your hand(s). For example, for 'spectacles' make round shapes with your thumbs and fingers and hold them against your eyes. If the sign represents a person, animal or toy special to your child, invent a movement or gesture that depicts a behaviour or feature particular to that person, animal or toy. Add as much mime and movement as possible to represent the action. Exaggerate your body language, and make dramatic facial expressions.

Most importantly, do not forget to document your new signs in your Invented signs page at the end of this section so that you can easily remember them. Show them to family members, friends and other caregivers who come into contact with your child. Be consistent when making a newly invented sign so as not to confuse your child!

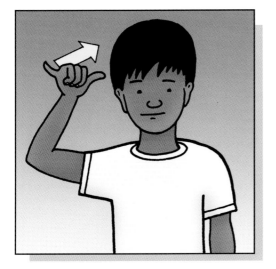

AEROPLANE

Close your middle three fingers into your palm leaving your little finger and thumb out (as wings). Fly your hand around like an aeroplane.

ALL GONE

Start with your fists together close to your chest, and then sweep both of them out and away from each other, opening your hands to flat.

ANGRY

Make your hands into a claw shape and hold them into your chest. Sharply move your hands up and down repeatedly, and adopt an angry facial expression.

ANIMAL

Use your arms and shoulders in a clawing motion, alternating your arms as if you were an animal walking.

BEE

Join the tips of your first finger and thumb to make an 'O' shape and then fly this around making a buzzing sound.

BIG

Stretch your arms wide apart to show that something is big.

BIRD/DUCK

Use the thumb and first two fingers on one hand to make a beak shape in front of your mouth.

For 'duck', make the beak at the side of your body.

BISCUIT

Claw one hand and tap it under the elbow of the other arm a few times.

BLANKET

Imagine you are using both hands to grab the top of a blanket, and pulling it up from your waist to your chin.

BOAT

Join the fingertips of both hands together and move your arms in a forward and wavy motion.

BOOK/STORY

Put your hands flat, palms together vertically, and open them out toward the horizontal as if opening a book.

BOY

Curl your fingers into your right hand leaving your index finger out. Move your finger flat under your chin from right to left.

BREAD

Put the edge of one hand on the other hand held flat, and 'slice' back and forwards.

BROTHER

Rub your two fists together in an alternating up-and-down motion.

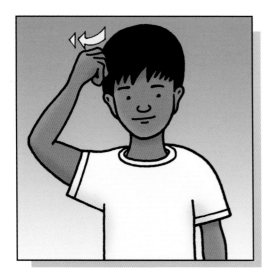

BRUSH HAIR

This is a mimed sign – so pretend to brush your hair.

BUCKET AND SPADE

Mime digging with a spade.

BUS

Imagine holding a large steering wheel: pretend you are driving.

BUTTERFLY

Link your two thumbs together and fan out the rest of your fingers and flap them as a butterfly would flap its wings.

CAKE

Cup your hand and tap while twisting it back and forth on your other flat palm a few times.

CAR

Pretend you are holding a car's steering wheel and make small steering movements.

CASTLE/SANDCASTLE

Move the first two fingers of each hand together in short up-and-down actions (as if drawing the outline of a castle) while raising your arms slightly.

CAT

With both hands grab imaginary whiskers and pull them away from your face.

CEREAL

Pretend to eat with a spoon, scooping the cereal up from the bowl to your mouth.

CHANGE

Clench your hands into fists, put your wrists together, and twist your hands alternately back and forth once.

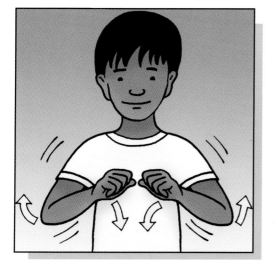

CHICKEN

Pretend your arms are wings, and flap them from the elbow up and down at the side of your body.

CLEAN

Wipe one flat hand over the other flat hand in a forward motion.

CLOTHES/GET DRESSED

Brush your open hands in an up and down motion, moving your arms slowly down from chest to waist.

COAT

Bring your hands down from your shoulders in front of you, to show putting on a coat

COLD

Hunch your shoulders and make fists with your hands, pumping them towards each other.

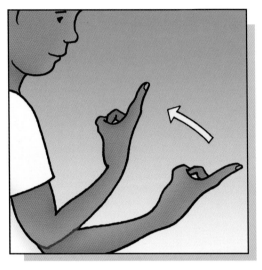

COME

Extend a pointed index finger and bring it back to point towards you.

COOK

Pretend you are stirring a bowl of food.

COUGH

Bang one clenched fist against your chest twice.

COW

Place one clenched fist above each ear, with just the little fingers extended upwards to depict the cow's horns.

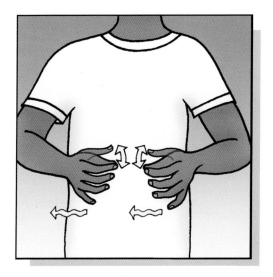

CRAB

Make your thumbs and fingers into pincers, thumbs touching, and move from left to right to show a crab walking sideways.

CREAM

Pretend you are rubbing cream with the fingers of one hand onto the top of the other hand.

CROCODILE

Stretch your arms out in front of you with one hand resting flat on top of the other, and open and close the flat hands like a crocodile's jaws.

CRY

Use both index fingers to follow the trail of tears alternately down your cheeks.

CUDDLE/HUG

Wrap your arms around your body to hug yourself.

DADDY/FATHER

Tap the two first fingers of one hand on the top of the two extended first fingers of the other hand. This is the fingerspell for 'F'.

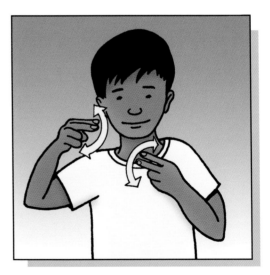

DANCE

Use the first two fingers of one hand in a V shape and wave them around. (You can do a little shimmy too.)

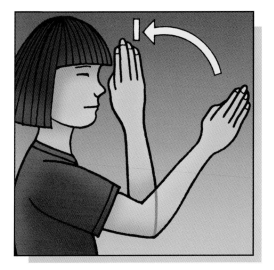

DANGER

With your flat palm facing sideways, sharply pull your hand up from an extended arm to meet your forehead.

DARK/NIGHT

Bring your forearms to cross each other in front of your body, stopping when they are level.

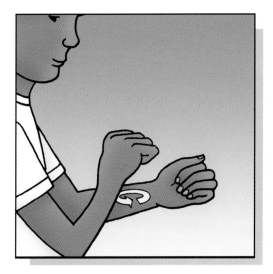

DIRTY

Close your hands crossed at the wrist, and rub the wrists against each other in small circles.

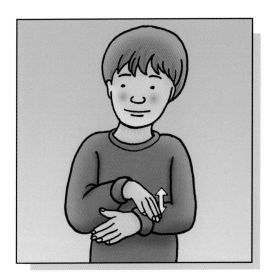

DOCTOR

Tap the tips of the index finger and thumb of one hand on the outside of the other wrist.

DOG

Point the first two fingers of both hands downwards, like a dog begging, and make small downward movements.

DON'T TOUCH/TOUCH – NO

Touch the fingertips of the first two fingers of one hand on the back of the other hand and shake your head, 'No'.

DOWN

Point downwards. (The opposite of 'up'.)

DRINK/JUICE

Cup your hand in front of and below your mouth, and tilt it back and forth in a drinking motion.

DRY

Rub the thumb of one hand from the pad of the little finger across the fingertips.

DUCK/BIRD

For Duck, make an open and closed beak motion at the side of your body using the thumb and first two fingers of one hand. For Bird, make the beak at the front of your mouth (as shown above).

EAT/FOOD

Bunch the fingers of one hand together and make little in-and-out movements by your mouth.

ELEPHANT

Start with your cupped hand by your face, and then move it down and out to depict the elephant's trunk.

FALL DOWN

Place the first two fingers of your right hand (to look like legs) pointing down onto the flat palm of your left hand, then twist the right hand and flop down so that the fingers lie flat on your palm.

FAMILY

Place the first two fingers of one hand on the backs of the first two fingers of the other hand, and move your hands round together in a small horizontal circle.

FARMER

Curl all your fingers into your hand except your thumb which touches the top of your chest. Move that hand down and away from the chest and then bring it back in again at the lower chest in an arch as if stretching braces on your trousers.

FINISHED

Do two thumbs-up and wave them around in small circular movements away from each other.

FIRE

Wiggle your fingers as your hands move up and down alternately.

FISH

Tilt one flat hand and wiggle it while moving forward like a fish swimming.

FLOWER

Touch the tips of your fingers together and pass them from one nostril to the other as if smelling a flower.

FOOD/EAT

Bunch the fingers of one hand together and make little in-and-out movements by your mouth.

FRIEND

Clasp one hand with the other and shake your own hand.

FULL

Bring a horizontally flat hand up from your chest to under your chin to show that you are full.

GARDEN/PARK

Tap one horizontally flat hand, palm down, against your upper chest twice.

GENTLE

With the fingers of one hand gently stroke the back of your other hand slowly.

GET DRESSED/CLOTHES

Brush your open hands in an up and down motion, moving your arms slowly down from chest to waist.

GET READY

With your hands open, tap your chest twice with your thumbs.

GIRAFFE

Place one hand at the base of your neck, with the neck between thumb and first finger, and then stroke upwards to your chin stretching your neck out.

GIRL/LADY/WOMAN

With the forefinger of one hand stroke the side of your face from ear to chin (to suggest the ribbon of a girl's bonnet). This is also the sign for 'pink'!

GO/LET'S GO

Move your hand forward away from your
body to show the direction you are going.

GOAT

Pull a clasped hand down from your chin
in a small movement.

GOOD

A simple thumbs-up!

GOOD (VERY), WELL DONE

Both thumbs up, moving each hand forward
in small, vertically circular movements.

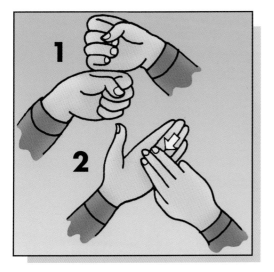

GRANDMA

Hands fingerspell 'G' and then 'M'.

Place one fist on top of the other fist (the fingerspell for 'G'), and then place the middle three fingers of one hand into the flat palm of the opposite hand (the fingerspell for 'M').

GRANDPA

Hands fingerspell 'G' and then 'F'.

Place one fist on top of the other fist (the fingerspell for 'G'), and then place the first two fingers of one hand on top of the first two fingers of the opposite hand (the fingerspell for 'F').

HAMSTER

Claw-shaped hands swivel back and forth on your cheeks to suggest a hamster's full cheeks.

HAPPY

Brush one horizontal palm against the other a couple of times – and remember to look happy!

HAT

Pull down an imaginary hat on both sides of the head.

HEAR/LISTEN/NOISE

Cup your hand to your ear.

HELP

Place one fist into the other hand held flat, and pull it towards you.

HIPPO

Put one downturned clenched fist on top of the upturned other, all knuckles facing forward, and open up from the wrists to suggest the hippo opening its mouth.

HOLIDAY

Place your hands flat against your head and then move them away and outwards, ending with your palms facing out.

HOME/HOUSE

Touch the fingertips of both hands together, keeping elbows apart to show the roof of a house.

HORSE

Place one fist on top of the other and move both forward in a small circle as if holding the horse's reins.

HOT

Move your clawed hand quickly from your mouth to one side.

HOUSE/HOME

Touch the fingertips of both hands together, keeping elbows apart to show the roof of a house.

HUG/CUDDLE

Wrap your arms around your upper body to hug yourself.

HURT/PAIN

Point to the area of pain and then shake your hands out.

ICE CREAM

Mime licking an ice cream cornet.

ILL

Hold both little fingers against your chest and drag them vertically down.

JUICE/DRINK

Cup your hand in front of and below your mouth, and tilt it back and forth in a drinking motion.

JUMP

Place the first two fingers of one hand (as legs) down onto the palm of the other hand, and jump them up and down.

LET'S GO/GO

Move your hand forward away from your body to show the direction you are going.

LIGHT/SUN

Open your fist above your head to suggest a light coming on.

LION

Bring a clawed hand over your head from one ear to the other to suggest the lion's mane.

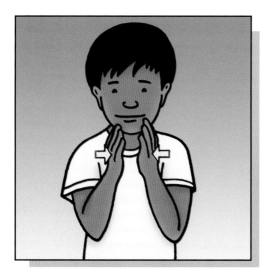

LITTLE/SMALL

Bring your hands together to suggest a small object.

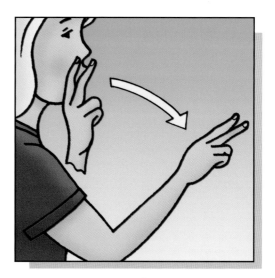

LOOK/SEE

Use the first two fingers of one hand in a V shape and direct them from your eyes to what you are looking at.

LOVE

Cross your hands over your heart.

ME

Point to yourself.

MEDICINE

Cup one hand and use the little finger of the other hand to stir around inside it.

MILK

Open and close one hand.

Note: This is a simplified version of the BSL sign – the correct sign is too difficult for babies to use.

MINE

Bring one fist to your chest.

MONKEY

Scratch under your armpits as a monkey does.

MOON

Draw the shape vertically with a thumb and index finger: with thumb and finger closed at the top, bring the arm down gradually opening the thumb and finger and closing them as you get to the bottom.

MORE

Pat one flat palm and fingers against the back of your other flat hand a few times.

MOUSE

Twist your index finger into the side of your nose.

MUMMY/MOTHER

Tap the middle three fingers of one hand on your forehead.

MUSIC

Act like a conductor.

NAPPY

Snap your fingers together at the sides of your body.

NIGHT/DARK

Bring your forearms to cross each other in front of your body, stopping when they are level.

OUT

With your right hand clasped and only the thumb up, twist the hand over to the right so the thumb points away from you.

OVER

Bring one hand over the other in an arch shape

PAIN/HURT

Point to the area of pain and then shake your hands out.

PARK/GARDEN

Tap one horizontally flat hand, palm down, against your upper chest twice.

PIG

Swivel one clasped hand over your nose a few times to suggest a pig's snout.

PLAY

With both hands palm up, make circular movements with the forearms while raising them.

PLEASE/THANK YOU

Touch your fingertips to your chin and then rotate your hand down and away from your body so that the hand finishes horizontal, palm up.

RABBIT

Put two fingers up each side of your head, as in rabbit ears.

RAIN

With your hands palms down, wiggle your fingers, moving your hands in and downwards.

RUN

Swing your arms forwards and backwards at the side of your body as if running.

SAD

Brush the side of your hand (thumb to nose) down your nose to your chest, and look sad.

SAND

Rub your fingers and thumbs together while raising your hands.

SANDCASTLE/CASTLE

Move the first two fingers of each hand together in short up-and-down actions (as if drawing the outline of a castle) while raising your arms slightly.

SAY/TELL

Move your index finger away from your mouth.

SCARED

Pull a clawed hand sharply away from your chest.

SEA

Use your arm to make a wavy motion from left to right.

SHARE

Put the edge of one hand on the palm of the other and slide it back and forth.

SHEEP

Place one clenched fist above each ear, with just the little fingers curling upwards to depict the sheep's curly horns.

SHOES

Cup one hand on top of the other hand, and move it along as if pulling on a shoe.

SHOP

With bent hands make two short downward movements.

SISTER

Hook your index finger over your nose and tap it twice.

SIT

Place one hand on top of the other and then move both hands down.

SLEEP

Your thumb and first finger act as your eyelids – close your index fingers onto your thumbs to mime closing your eyes.

SLIDE

Whoosh one hand down in a swooping motion.

SMALL/LITTLE

Bring your hands together to suggest a small object.

SMELLY

Wave your hand in front of your wrinkled nose.

SNAKE

Use the thumb and first two fingers of one hand to form a fork tongue, and slide it forward in a slithering motion.

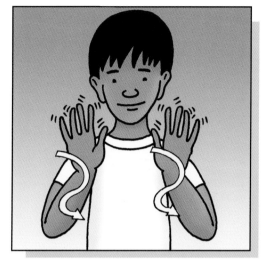

SNOW

Flutter your fingers and move your hands down in a slow zigzag motion

SOAP

Rub your hands together in circular movements as if you were washing them.

SOCKS

Mime pulling your socks up.

SORRY

Move one fist in a circular movement around your chest.

SPIDER

Wiggle the fingers of a claw-shaped hand.

STAND

Place the tips of the first two fingers of one hand down into the palm of the opposite hand.

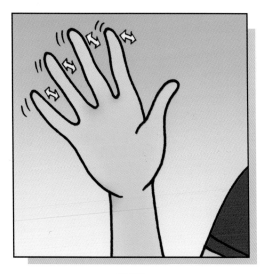

STAR

Put your hand in the air, palm facing forward, and wiggle your fingers.

STOP/WAIT

Quickly put both hands out in front of you, palms facing vertically forward.

SUN/LIGHT

Open your fist above your head to suggest a light coming on.

SWIM

Do the breast-stroke with your arms.

SWING

Swing your arms back and forth by the sides of your body.

TELEPHONE

Mime holding a phone to your ear.

TELEVISION

Draw a box outline in the air with your first finger of each hand.

TELL/SAY

Move your index finger away from your mouth.

TIGER

Put both hands in a claw shape over your face and pull them out to show the stripes and claws.

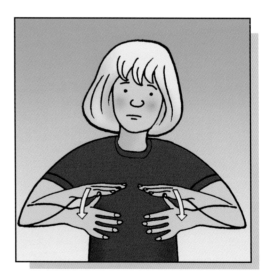

TIRED

Hold your hands flat in front of you with your thumbs touching your chest, and then rotate your hands down flat against you, keeping the thumbs where they are.

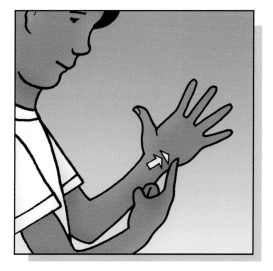

TOILET

Tap the index finger of one hand on the outside edge of the other hand. This is the fingerspell for 'T'.

TOOTHBRUSH/BRUSH TEETH

Pretend to brush your teeth.

TOUCH – NO/DON'T TOUCH

Touch the fingertips of the first two fingers of one hand on the back of the other hand and shake your head, 'No'.

TOWEL

Pretend you are drying the back of your neck with a towel.

TRAIN

With your forearm horizontal, move your hand in circles at the side of your body to mimic an old fashioned steam train.

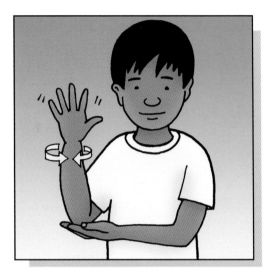

TREE

Place one elbow on the flat palm of the other hand. Keep the upper hand in the air and spread your fingers. You can wave it around a little.

UNDER

Sweep one hand under the other.

UP

Point your index finger upwards.

WAKE UP/AWAKE

Your thumbs and first fingers act as your eyelids – flick the fingers up from the thumbs in front of your eyes to mime opening your eyes.

WAIT/STOP

Put both hands out in front of you, palms facing vertically forward.

WALK

Let the first two fingers of one hand do the walking.

WANT

Put your hand flat against your chest and then sweep it out, twisting your palm down.

WARM

Move a clawed hand slowly in a small circle to the side of your mouth.

WASH FACE

Pretend to wash your face by rubbing both hands over it.

WATER

Put the thumb and index finger of one hand together and move from your ear down to your mouth.

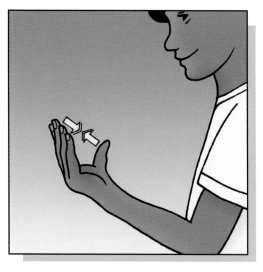

WET

Close and open your fingers on to your thumb a few times. You can use one or two hands.

WHERE?

Turn both hands palm up, and move them in small outward circles.

WHICH?

Stick your thumb and little finger out, curling the other fingers into your hand, then move your hand from side to side.

WIND

Blow with your mouth, using sweeping movements with your arms to show the direction the wind is blowing.

WORK

Chop the edge of one flat hand down onto the edge of the other at right angles.

A - Z of signs

WORM

Wiggle your index finger forwards.

YOU

Point at the person addressed.

My invented signs

The next three pages are left blank for you to record any signs that you have invented yourself.

You should list three parts to each sign: the sign's hand-shape, the sign's location in relation to the body, and the sign's movement.

References and further reading

Acredolo, Linda and Goodwyn, Susan (2000) Baby Signs. Vermillion, London.

Daniels, Dr Marilyn (2001) Dancing with Words: Signing for Hearing Children's Literacy. Bergin & Garvey, Westport, Connecticut.

Smith, Cath (1990) Signs Make Sense. Souvenir Press, London.

Ward, Dr Sally (2004) Baby Talk. Arrow Books, London.

Accelerates speech in babies

Acredolo, Linda and Goodwyn, Susan (1997) 'Furthering our understanding of what humans understand', in Human Development, 40, pp.25–31.

Goodwyn, Susan and Acredolo, Linda (1993) 'Symbolic gesture versus word: Is there a modality advantage for onset of symbol use?', in Child Development, 64, pp.688–701.

Moore, B., Acredolo L. P. and Goodwyn, S. W. (2001) 'Symbolic gesturing and joint attention: Partners in facilitating verbal development', Paper presented at the Biennial Meetings of the Society for Research in Child Development, April.

A greater written and spoken vocabulary

Daniels, Marilyn (1994a) 'The effects of sign language on hearing children's language development', in Communication Education, 43, pp.291–8, October.

Daniels, Marilyn (1996) 'Seeing language: The effect over time of sign language on vocabulary development in early childhood education', in Child Study Journal, 26, pp.193–208.

Felzer, L. (1998) 'A multisensory reading program that really works', in Teaching and Change, 5, pp.169–83.

Hafer, J. (1986) Signing for Reading Success. Clerc Books, Gallaudet University Press, Washington DC.

Koehler, L. and Loyd, L. (1986) 'Using finger spelling/manual signs to facilitate reading and spelling', Paper presented at the Biennial Conference of the International Society for Augmentative and Alternative Communication, Cardiff, Wales, September.

Wilson, R., Teague, J. and Teague, M. (1985) 'The use of signing and fingerspelling to improve spelling performance with hearing children', in Reading Psychology, 4, pp.267–73.

A higher IQ

Acredolo, Linda and Goodwyn, Susan (2000) 'The long-term impact of symbolic gesturing during infancy on IQ at age 8', Paper presented at the meetings of the International Society for Infant Studies, Brighton, UK, July.

Goodwyn, S. W., Acredolo L. P. and Brown, C. (2000) 'The impact of symbolic gesturing on early language development', in Journal of Nonverbal Behaviour, 24, pp.81–103.

Moore, B., Acredolo, L. P. and Goodwyn, S. W. (2001) 'Symbolic gesturing and joint attention: Partners in facilitating verbal development', Paper presented at the Biennial Meetings of the Society for Research in Child Development, April.

Increased brain activity

Acredolo, Linda and Goodwyn, Susan (1988) 'Symbolic gesturing in normal infants', in Child Development, 59, pp.450–66.

Acredolo, Linda and Goodwyn, Susan (1990) 'The significance of symbolic gesturing for understanding language development', in R. Vasta (ed.) Annals of Child Development, 7, Jessica Kingsley Publishers, London, pp.1–42.

Acredolo, L., Goodwyn, S., Horobin, K. and Emmons, Y. (1999) 'The signs and sounds of early language development', in L. Balter and C. Tamis-LeMonda (eds) Child Psychology: A Handbook of Contemporary Issues, Psychology Press, New York, pp.116–39.

Bavelier, D., Corina, D. P. and Neville, H. J. (1998) 'Brain and language: a perspective from sign language', in Neuron, Vol.21, Cell Press, August, pp.275–8.

Calvin, W. H. and Ojemann, G. A. (1980) Inside the Brain: Mapping the Cortex, Exploring the Neuron. New American Library.

Baby signing and a baby's development

Goodwyn, Susan and Acredolo, Linda (1998) 'Encouraging symbolic gestures: Effects on the relationship between gesture and speech', in J. Iverson and S. Goldin-Meadow (eds) The Nature and Functions of Gesture in Children's Communication, Jossey-Bass, San Francisco, pp.61–73.

Griffith, P. L. (1985) 'Mode-switching and mode-finding in a hearing child of deaf parents', in Sign Language Studies, 48, pp.195–222.

Karmiloff-Smith, A. (1995) 'The extraordinary journey from foetus through infancy', in Journal of Child Psychology and Psychiatry, 36, pp.1,293–315.

Wilbur, R. and Jones, M. (1974) 'Some aspects of the acquisition of American Sign Language and English by three hearing children of deaf parents', in M. W. LaGaly, R. A. Fox and A. Bruck (eds), Papers from the Tenth Regional Meeting of the Chicago Linguistic Society.

Signing and children with special needs

Apraxia of speech

Square, P. A. (1994) 'Treatment approaches for developmental apraxia of speech', in Clinical Communication Disorders, 4 (3), September, pp.151–61.

Down's syndrome

Donovan, C.-L. P. (1998) 'Teaching sign language', in Disability Solutions, Vol.2, Issue 5, January/February.

Gibbs, E. D., Springer, A. S., Cooley, S. C. and Aloisio, S. (1991) 'Early use of total communication: Patterns across eleven children with Down's syndrome', Paper presented at the International Early Childhood Conference on Children with Special Needs, St Louis, MO, November.

Hopmann, M. R. (1993) 'The use of signs by children with Down's syndrome', in Down's Syndrome Today, Vol.2, No.2, pp.22–3.

Miller, J. F., Sedey, A., Miolo, G., Rosin, M. and Murray-Branch, J. (1992) 'Vocabulary acquisition in young children with Down's syndrome: Speech and sign', Paper presented at the 9th World Congress of the International Association for the Scientific Study of Mental Deficiency, Queensland, Australia, August.

Reading disabilities

Blackburn, D., Vonvillian, J. and Ashby, R. (1984) 'Manual communication as an alternative mode of language instruction for children with severe reading disabilities', in Language, Speech and Hearing Services in Schools, 15, January, pp.22–31.

Carney, J., Cioffi, G. and Raymond, W. (1985) 'Using sign language for teaching sight words', in Teaching Exceptional Children, Spring, pp.214–17.

Sensenig, L., Topf, B. and Mazeika, E. (1989) 'Sign language facilitation of reading with students classified as trainable mentally handicapped', in Education and Training of the Mentally Retarded, June, pp.121–5.

Vernon, M., Coley, J., Hafer, J. and Dubois, J. (1980) 'Using sign language to remediate severe reading problems', in Journal of Learning Disabilities, 13, April, pp.215–18.

Notes

The DVD dictionary

Emma Finlay-Smith, founder of the Babysigners teaching network, demonstrates each sign included in this book.

The DVD is alphabetically indexed for easy access.

baby signers

www.babysigners.co.uk